the disconnected man

the disconnected man

breaking down walls and restoring intimacy with him

jim turner

New York   Nashville

FaithWords
Hachette Book Group
1290 Avenue of the Americas, New York, NY 10104
faithwords.com
twitter.com/faithwords

First Edition: December 2017

FaithWords is a division of Hachette Book Group, Inc. The FaithWords name and logo are trademarks of Hachette Book Group, Inc.

The publisher is not responsible for websites (or their content) that are not owned by the publisher.

The Hachette Speakers Bureau provides a wide range of authors for speaking events. To find out more, go to www.hachettespeakersbureau.com or call (866) 376-6591.

LCCN: 2017950960

ISBNs: 978-1-4789-7564-9 (hardcover), 978-1-4789-7563-2 (ebook)

Printed in the United States of America

LSC-C

10 9 8 7 6 5 4 3 2 1

I would like to dedicate this book to every man who finds the courage to connect and every woman who has the courage to endure until that day arrives. May you delight in each other as God delights in you.

Contents

the disconnected man

What Does *Disconnected* Mean?

I suspect you know. As soon as you heard the title, it probably rang a bell for you, or sparked a memory, or touched that part of you that has always sought a definition—a definition for the man who leaves your mind in a conundrum when you try to figure out why he is the way he is.

Our culture might define him as the "strong, silent type" or the "lone wolf." That's not really accurate. To an outside observer, those terms might seem to fit well, but they lack depth; they don't pursue the man beyond his surface persona. You might have been tempted to define him this way yourself. But somewhere deep inside, you realized that those phrases just don't work. Something keeps nagging you to find a better definition or explanation for him. Your heart won't let your mind pigeonhole him that easily.

You know that the word *disconnected* fits him, but you may not know all the reasons why. Try using the word with someone else who knows him well. I do this often when I talk to people about "this man."

When you use the word *disconnected* in reference to this man in your life—especially if the person you're talking to knows him as well, something remarkable happens. Your friend or family member will react. That reaction and the observations that follow will tell you if you've hit the mark. I've found time after time that those who know a man like this find that *disconnected* works to describe him. There's no better word. Your conversation will reveal why this word fits so well.

Nearly everyone I meet knows a man they can apply the word *disconnected* to. They have observed him, tried to get to know him, perhaps been hurt by him, and have an opinion about what makes him that way. Many of the opinions you will hear others express about this man are insightful, but they rarely get to the core.

One of the reasons you will still be left grasping for answers is because the best person to define what *disconnected* means is the disconnected man himself. Problem is, he's not saying anything.

One of the foundational traits of the disconnected man is that he usually doesn't know he's disconnected. He wouldn't even think to give you a description. He is unaware that you are even searching for one. I suppose that's where I come in. I'm a formerly disconnected, now struggling-to-be-connected, man. Like your man, I didn't have a clue that I was disconnected. Having been there before, and now being able to look back, gives me a window into his soul you might not have. I can tell you a few of his secrets.

Before I do, though, let's continue to consider: Who is this disconnected man? The man you're thinking of is probably a fairly happy guy, competent in tasks he takes on, relatively unemotional, usually enjoyable to be around, capable of carrying heavy loads of responsibility. But he's very difficult to get to know more deeply. If he is your friend, the friendship is most likely superficial. You get a certain sense around him. Your heart whispers questions such as, *Am I important to him? Does he know how I feel? Why can't I seem to keep his attention?* and many more. The nature of a disconnected man often leaves you wondering, *Am I the problem?*

The answer is—probably not. If you recognize these as observations you've made about the man you know, if these words resonate with you, if your heart and mind detect some truth here, then you are probably *not* the cause of the problem. In addition, you are probably not the only one to suspect that there's something different about this man. Knowing that you are not the problem may not help you resolve the riddle, but I hope it helps you rest a bit more easy about your relationship with him.

In fact, not only are you not the problem, but you are also probably very important to your disconnected man—maybe more important than anyone else has ever been. If that surprises you or sounds unbelievable, please don't dismiss the statement as impossible. It may very well be the truest truth you'll ever be surprised by.

One of the most difficult barriers to believing that you are important to your disconnected man is that you don't see it or feel it from him. He has a way of looking through you. When you look in his eyes, you don't see yourself. It's sort of blank in there. There's no swirl of emotion, no tide of understanding, no link with your heart, and no tangible reaction to your outreach. It's discouraging, perhaps devastating, to experience this complete lack of connection. But did you know that he *doesn't* know that you feel disconnected? Did you know that he *thinks* he's connecting? He would actually be surprised and a bit confused if he could see your frustration. I mean, if he could see your *real* frustration. He thinks your frustration is about something completely unrelated to what's actually bothering you.

So what is really happening here?

Picture an impenetrable wall: tall, shiny, black, with no door. In front of it is a happy-go-lucky, easygoing mind. This is your disconnected man's normal, outward appearance. The mind in front of the wall is where he lives 98 percent of the time. It's a state of blissful blindness. But behind the wall is a place that is very real but seldom visited, housing a storm of thoughts and feelings. There's a rich world of meaning and a fragile emotional stability just beyond that blank surface. You see it when he attempts to explain the way he feels. He stumbles and becomes frustrated because the meaning is there but he doesn't have the emotional language to communicate it. You get a glimpse when he breaks down into uncontrollable emotion, perhaps over something you don't feel is extremely emotional—a movie scene, a story, a moment of closeness. It's very difficult for him when that wall is breached even a little. He finds himself awash in confusion and embarrassment when something touches that sensitive place behind the wall. You've probably suspected it was there but didn't know you were seeing it.

The wall is carefully crafted (or not so carefully) to look like confidence or happiness. The amazing thing is that the disconnected man doesn't even know the wall is there, so he's not looking for the door. Behind that wall is everything worth knowing about this man. So how do you get on the other side? And what happens if you get there?

If he were aware of that inner world, the disconnected man would probably be mortified that it even exists and that you want to go there. He's not like you. You are capable of going to places he doesn't know about. The reality is that you live in a foreign land of feelings and emotions and connection that he doesn't know he's supposed to be a part of. You move in and out of relational realities that are veiled to him. You feel. You identify. You share. You know depression. You know elation. You connect deeply. You intuit friendship. You let love fill you up. You grieve. You are naturally touched by a thousand relational realities. The disconnected man is not. At least not in the same way you are.

Let me illustrate. Did you know that a shark can sense a slight ripple in the current from miles away? It can sense tiny temperature changes rising from great depths. Some sharks can detect blood in the water at one part per 10 billion—that's one drop in an Olympic-sized swimming pool. The shark is specially fitted for success in its environment. You are specially fitted for success in your relational environment. You are a relational shark. On the other hand, the disconnected man is like a lion dropped into an ocean. He is powerful in his own environment but helpless in yours. He might be able to swim for a while, but he can't make sense of his surroundings. He can't detect the ripples or temperature or the presence of food. Regardless of his strength, after a short time he will eventually flail around in frustration, then withdraw, and then give up. I imagine you've seen this pattern. We'll explore it in more detail later in the book.

So there he is: a lion in the ocean. But what defines him? What is a disconnected man?

A disconnected man is one who is unaware that he is nonrelational, distant, and emotionally unavailable.

The key to this definition is that he is *unaware* of his position. He thinks he's relational. He thinks he comes across as caring and interested. He thinks he's connected. His oblivious nature is what makes reaching him so difficult. You, on the other hand, are keenly aware of his disconnection. You may have tried every way you know to reach him or try to understand him, but you failed—not from lack of trying, either. You failed because your disconnected man is relationally blind.

So, how do you get on the other side of his wall? And how can he learn to thrive in an unnatural environment? *How do you help him see himself?* It's the question every person who knows a disconnected man should be asking. It will lead you to the combination that unlocks his heart and frees him for relationship!

But first, I have a question for you: Do you care enough about this man to fight for him? Are you strong enough to be his friend (or spouse, as the case may be)?

I ask these questions as a warning because reaching your disconnected man will not be easy. You may be in for a protracted battle with fierce opposition: He doesn't think anything is wrong with him and doesn't know why you are so hurt. If you are not careful, he will be offended (and probably angry) that you are trying to "fix" him. He probably won't deliberately fight you but he will be frustrated, because he doesn't realize there's a battle going on. His wall is high and it is guarded by hidden and relentless forces entrenched deep in his psyche. These are forces of pride and emotional protection and the comfort of not having to connect. They are buried so deep that he doesn't suspect them of being there. But they will come out in his responses (or lack thereof), his reactions to probing, his perception of reality, his vulnerability to criticism, and perhaps a hundred other ways.

Fighting this kind of battle is intense, and it demands a tremendous amount of wisdom and patience. But since your disconnected man doesn't know his dilemma, he can't possibly know that you have entered into combat to break through his disconnection and free him up for real relationship. He's like a happy child playing on the seashore while a raging tide is pulling you under. I'm not trying to be dramatic here—the reality of working with a disconnected man can truly be this severe. We will explore this battle in detail as we go on.

A dear friend of mine who was dealing with a disconnected man asked me, "What's the difference between a narcissist and a disconnected man?" She was struggling with a common misperception, because from the outside looking in, narcissism and disconnection are not much different. In reality, they are quite different.

To clarify further what *disconnected* means, let's look at what it doesn't mean. The Encyclopedia Britannica defines narcissism as a pathological self-absorption: "Narcissism is characterized by an inflated self-image and addiction to fantasy, by an unusual coolness and composure shaken only when the narcissistic confidence is threatened, and by the tendency to take others for granted or to exploit them." A narcissist wants nothing more than to satisfy himself at any cost, and he doesn't care if people get hurt while he does it.

A disconnected man, on the other hand, already feels satisfied within himself, and he believes he's meeting the needs of others by his hard work and faithfulness. He doesn't feel a pressing need for relational connection, so he can't identify with those who are not getting it from him. He is not focused on his own need, as a narcissist is. He is simply unaware that others have needs he could and perhaps should meet but isn't. He is also unaware that he has very deep unmet needs himself, because that part of him is buried. *A disconnected man hurts people because he doesn't have the equipment to connect with them. A narcissist hurts people because he uses them for his own gratification.*

Another common conclusion made about the disconnected man is that he is indifferent or uncaring. This description seems to fit him, because he's so distant and so easily able to switch gears and get back to work or move on to whatever it is he's doing. Neither grief nor elation last long for him, because the wall we spoke of earlier makes it impossible for emotions to sink all the way in and last. So it seems that he lacks depth because he's so unaffected by emotional issues. This was me to a T.

One clear example of this was when my dad died. I loved my father dearly, but if you had observed my reactions when he passed away, you may not have believed that I cared. I showed very little emotion throughout his illness, his suffering, and his death. I don't actually remember feeling a lot of emotion. What little emotion did surface didn't last. I got back to life as I knew it quickly and easily. I cared superficially that my dad had died, but I couldn't connect with the deeper emotional loss that others around me were feeling.

While it's true that he's unemotional, make no mistake, your disconnected man really does care. It's just that his ability to express care and concern keeps bouncing off that thick wall. If he thinks you are lacking anything to make you comfortable, he will gladly work harder to give you whatever thing (clothing, a comfortable home, good food, flowers, chocolates, etc.) he imagines will fulfill you. But he will never think to try to connect more deeply with your heart. He desires to overcome any obstacle blocking your happiness, but he truly doesn't see that the real obstacle is his own disconnection.

Has this definition of disconnection surprised you? Do you struggle with understanding how anyone can be so unaware of his own relational and emotional surroundings? Is it hard for you to accept that your disconnected man's inattention is not intentional? If so, it might help you to know how he got this way. I've got some ideas based on my own previous disconnection.

Chapter 1

How Did He Get This Way?

There are several paths to disconnection, but the dynamic works like this: Negative experiences cause internal closure.

Something happens to this man, or boy, that his mind or soul responds negatively to. Whatever the negative experience, his response is to close down or block off part of his heart because that negative stimulus makes him uncomfortable or even hurts him deeply. The experience either caused pain or failed to relieve his pain. For instance, if a boy is abused and made to feel pain, he might block out that experience and his emotional response. If a man is ignored, untouched, or not verbally affirmed, he might block out the need for connection, deciding that he doesn't need those affirmations.

There are many variations and levels of intensity to these negative external stimuli, and just as many effects on different personality types, but the net effect is that the boy or man is emotionally damaged. He becomes a guarded man, one who probably doesn't even know about the shield around his heart. He may appear normal and healthy from any outward assessment. He may be responsible (hardworking, doing his duty), reliable (doing things for others, showing up on time), giving (always willing to give things or money to others), and possessed of many other admirable traits. Or he may have simply given up, becoming lazy, unreliable, and self-absorbed—settling for mediocrity. Regardless of his response to the negative experiences, what you see is his inability to connect with the people in his life.

But why?

Disconnected men have happy, locked-up hearts.

Disconnected men typically seem to be happy, carefree, and lighthearted because they have an incredible capacity for stuffing things into emotional boxes or locking them into encrypted vaults that no one has the code to. I know this because I lived it. I was a master encoder of my emotions—so good that no one could crack my security. All my hurts, insecurities, and anxieties were guarded so safely that even *I* couldn't break in and access them. It was as if I had devised a hideously complex security code and then completely forgotten how to decipher it.

Everything emotional in my life was so securely locked away that my heart was like one big empty mausoleum of dead feelings. Even when I wanted to feel something, I often found myself wandering around in an echo chamber of lost sentiment. On the few occasions that something got through and touched my tender emotions, I ended up sobbing uncontrollably. This made me very uncomfortable. I felt as if I needed to be grasped and held together or I would fall apart. Even as I write this, I'm craving some great strong embrace to weep into, some tangible, loving, fatherly hug to drive away all my fears while I fall apart. I've felt this many times since the day God revealed to me who I really was. (I'll share that story later.) But it's a good thing I can feel it now. In the past I didn't want to fall apart, but now I do.

You might be thinking that there is no way a person could be happy with all their emotions impenetrably locked down. The fascinating thing is that I was only keeping the negative, hurtful, anxious, tender, and vulnerable emotions locked down. My positive, productive, "happy" feelings were free to run and play. My heart was a blissful Pollyanna of blind optimism. I was living in a sort of utopian dream, where some entity kept painting roses and daffodils on the huge canvas that was hiding all the pain and reality I should have been seeing. The ignorant flowers made me so happy.

Once that canvas gets moved aside, the disconnected man will experience an unraveling of tangled emotions. Discovering my own disconnection was a deeply unnerving experience. The unraveling left me feeling helpless and undone, but I have to admit I needed to feel that way. It was the only thing that could have broken the cables that bound me to my emotionless, empty bliss. It was a soul-meltdown for me—I was confronted with the brute force of a self-destroying truth. I then had to ask myself: Am I willing to allow God to put His finger on my need? I was staring into the blazing fire of His love. He was asking me if I was willing to walk with Him into the void of my heart and feel the extent of the vacuum. He was interrogating my newly alive realization, my awareness of my deep need for connection, to learn if I trusted Him enough to allow Him to heal me. I knew that road was for me—no one else could walk it for me. I knew that if I didn't walk it, I would never be able to help anyone else walk it. I also knew that if I couldn't walk that path, then I couldn't be a real man in any true, godly sense of the word.

How did all this get started for me?

I ran into the perfect storm of intentionally relational people at the same time that the closest relationship I had ever known was falling apart. The combination of having those relational people who loved me demand that I love them back, coupled with the pain of a failing relationship, threw me out of my comfortably sailing but emotionless boat into a raging, passionate sea. The lion had to learn to swim. Relationships would no longer wait. It was swim or die, relate or retreat.

This storm was an echo of the relational nature of God reflected in those created in His image—an echo that had finally caught up with me. I had to pay attention to the echo and to those who were the sounding boards of the echo. Prior to that time in my life, though, they were only faint whispers in my subconscious. Had I met with those people or paid attention to those echoes earlier, I might not have spent so much of my life hurting those who were looking to me to meet their needs for connection. If someone in my life could have brought me face-to-face with my relational self, I might have been able to avoid the disaster that inevitably followed my inability to connect. I think many tried, but I was utterly unable to respond to their efforts.

Let me tell you what happened to me as I wrote the paragraph above: I broke down and bawled. I want so badly to be that strong embrace for others. My soul is crying out for lives to pour myself into. I have experienced the walk into the caverns of my heart with God. Having been down there and back, I now know that I have to encourage others to take that terrible trek.

As a man, I have an obligation to be a fountainhead of love, encouragement, grace, passion, and blessing to everyone God brings within my sphere. Before my experience, I failed miserably at this. To have any hopes of becoming a man like this, I had to enter into the abyss of my own making. I had to take God's hand and allow Him to drag me through a black mire of suffocating pain. I had to feel the compression of a thousand fears, seemingly pressing the last breath from my gasping soul. My mind, at times, seemed to splinter into a million scattered failures and then fall to the ground in flames. The pressure that these dark realities brought nearly exploded my heart. I begged to be set free. I pleaded with my conscience to release me from the onslaught of my own guilt, but God did not allow it until I was completely incinerated. I was then able to entertain the hope of coming out clean. I saw that I had a chance to emerge holy. I could arise from the ashes of my purging to become a man striving for resolute character, fullness of life, power in grace, boldness in blessing, fearless in sacrifice, and boundless in love—a connected man.

But did I want to be that man badly enough to go through

the hell of having my old self die? I often wanted (and am still tempted) to shrink back into the comfortable emptiness of an emotionless existence. I have to remind myself to open my heart to the salt of painful, yet delicious relational connections. And I'm often reminded that my choice could mean someone's salvation, someone's deliverance.

That longing to love and be loved has been a shadowy, distant, but real presence to me. Even when I was mostly numb to emotions, I could see out of the corner of my soul's eye the reflection of something bright and warm. I have always wanted companionship and to be a harbor for hearts that needed safety, but these worthy goals eluded me through the years.

I'm convinced that there are many, many men (and perhaps some women) who could repeat this description and track it through their adult failures. The thought of those men, and the women who love them, is what compelled me to write this book. How many of us can characterize ourselves as happy and healthy but with no capacity for intimacy or deep emotional attachment? Are we in some sort of danger? Yes, we are. The danger may not seem imminent—in fact, we may not ever feel it until it's much too late. The danger is that there are probably dearly loved spouses, children, and friends throwing themselves against the emotionless walls of our cheery exteriors, only to be battered and broken like rag dolls in a tempest.

I want to encourage the women who love men like me that there is hope for you and for your relationship with your disconnected man. In Chapter 5, "Walls You Can't See," there is a Disconnection versus Intimacy test. It's a series of questions that I developed after discovering what was truly driving me when I was disconnected. They will help the disconnected man determine if he is intimacy-challenged. My advice is for men to answer these questions for themselves, and then ask their wives and close friends to answer from the standpoint of an outsider looking into the man's life. If you care and if you dare, you will become vulnerable and take the test and ask your loved ones to join you. It won't be easy, but if you want to let go of your disconnectedness and live for God and others, you need to face the truth. (Please resist the urge to take the test now; you should first read these earlier chapters.)

I thought long and hard about trying to track where my disconnection started. I mentally paced back through my childhood, teens, and young adulthood. These memories were somewhat relevant, but they still didn't answer the ultimate question of how I grew to be disconnected. I concluded that it doesn't take a crisis or serious abuse to affect a man at his heart level.

Small things, oft repeated, can sometimes do more damage than single traumas.

It may or may not matter when your disconnection started. It might have been as a boy or a man. Everyone's experience is different and everyone's disconnection is different. You might have suffered a great deal more pain early on or less pain early with a traumatic event later. Regardless of how your disconnection developed, it's there now, and it needs to be addressed.

It may help you to retrace the steps that led you to be disconnected; then again, it may not. Everyone is different. Some of you will need to explore every nuance of your life's journey to discover what shut down your heart. Some of you will need to simply pick up where you are because the pain is too real to go back. Some of you will need help from others with the path ahead, where some of you will only need to know that the term *disconnected* describes you—God will do the rest as you wrestle alone with this newfound narrative of your life. Either way, I invite you to read your own story and ask yourself how it's going and how you want it to end.

In contrast to the disconnected man, there may be those reading this book as healthy, relational people who are in relationships with disconnected men. My first encouragement to you is to pray. You may be tempted after reading this book to run to this man and tell him that you now know what's wrong with him. I'm not saying you won't be tactful when you tell him; I'm warning you that if you get excited about the fact that you've found help in this book and feel the urge to go tell him, he probably won't receive it very well. It could backfire on you. So slow down, give it time, pray a lot, and ask for God's timing. God cares about you and He cares about your man. If you are reading this, then God is intending to do work in your heart and possibly in your man's heart. Be patient—let God do the work.

It is so important that *God* speak to your man's heart. The Holy Spirit has a way of penetrating his wall that you may never find the words to do. Asking your disconnected man to read this book could, for him, actually be a very *negative* approach. There are a lot of hints in coming chapters about how to love this man out of his disconnection. Read them and meditate on them before you attempt any changes. It took a long time for him to become the man he is. So it's okay for you to take the necessary time to let God work. (Don't worry, it won't take as long as it took for him to become disconnected; God wants him healed and whole even more than you do.)

FOR FURTHER CONTEMPLATION

Negative experiences in a man's life often cause him to close his heart off to emotional connection and relational understanding. Do you know someone like this? If so, how do you think his disconnection affects those around him? If you're in a relationship with a disconnected man, how does that make you feel? What struggles and questions do you and his friends and loved ones wrestle with? What *really* happens to you when you are desperately trying to connect with your disconnected man? You may already be able to answer these questions easily, and the next chapter might be about you—the person who loves the disconnected man.

Chapter 2

Disconnection Meets Disaster

A disconnected man has the ability to emotionally (and often physically) "walk away" from relationships without much memory, regret, or feeling of loss. A disconnected man who is a Christian can do this too. But his convictions often keep him from physically walking away, especially in his marriage. Further, a disconnected man may feel that his marriage *is* connected and intimate so he wouldn't even think of walking away. He probably feels very secure in it, especially if his wife doesn't challenge his lack of emotional intimacy. He is capable of trotting effortlessly through life without the weight of emotional baggage, so if there's even a hint of a relationship, it satisfies him. As long as his family is together and he's meeting their needs and they get along, he will generally say that everything is great, even when it's often all a sham.

Not that he sees it as a sham—he doesn't detect the void. But just ask his wife. Asking the person closest to him will often reveal a world of intense pain and confusion—a world that he was unaware existed. The contrast between what the disconnected man feels compared to what those who love him feel is stark. The two are so diametrically opposed as to make it nearly impossible for either party to understand the other. His wife and other loved ones see a man who is profoundly relationally broken, even while the disconnected man sees himself as stable and happy.

I was that man. If you had asked me about my marriage, I would have said that it was great. I had good kids who were following the Lord, I was involved in a great ministry, and God was providing all our needs. My wife and I got along and she seemed to be happy. We didn't fight and, when we did have a disagreement, we usually worked it out fairly quickly. It all seemed good to me. Until the day my wife left, never to return. Hearing our story may help you understand how someone who tries to love a disconnected man *really* feels.

I could recount the history of our relationship, but I want to get right to the point. Trying to track the progression of the deterioration of our relationship would only be a distraction. I didn't know it, but during all the years of our marriage, my wife was suffering in silence. She tried to tell me in every way she knew how, but I was deaf to her pleas. I heard them very faintly, but there was nothing in me to answer them. It was like hearing a distant cry for help but with no way to detect what direction it was coming from or what was needed even if I could get there.

The truth is that my wife had been throwing herself against

the walls of my emotional Gibraltar for years and had become so battered and exhausted from trying to break through that she couldn't see the point of continuing the attempt. I don't know what this looked like to her. I was still mostly disconnected and couldn't really understand the emotion and where it was coming from or what caused it. I got a glimpse of it only when we went to counseling in the last days of our marriage and I heard the depth of her pain and frustration. I was so shocked that I don't remember much of anything she said— only that she was done with me. Add to this that I had become bitter with her about things that were minor at best (although major to me in my bitterness). I blew up in anger several times with her when pressures were high and my nagging bitterness erupted to the surface. These, along with the stresses of marriage to a man with no ability to relate, proved too much for her. She gave up, divorced me, and moved on.

May I speak to my dear Christian sisters here? I may have just described your man, or you may recognize some traits that strike close to your pain. You may have been tempted to take the extreme action my wife did. You might even be thinking of it now. I encourage you to read on before you do. This might describe what you are experiencing at the moment, but your relationship doesn't have to stay this way. You can play a big role in moving your man toward emotional intimacy.

I don't want to speak for my ex-wife, but I need to let you know what I heard in the days we were trying to reconcile and find a way forward. I want to stress that this is from *my* perspective—this is what sticks in my mind and heart from the counseling sessions and conversations we had after everything started to fall apart. These are the things she said to me that revealed the depth of her pain. It was too late for our relationship when she was finally able to say these things. If any of them sound familiar, I want to beg you, husband or wife, drop to your knees now and cry out to the Lord for discernment on what to do with them.

How does a woman feel when her husband is incapable of emotional connection? I would encourage husbands to ask themselves this, but I know that if you are disconnected and reading this you probably can't come up with an accurate answer. *But the accurate answer is exactly what you need.* Not the intellectual *facts* of the answer, but the shattered and raw, relationally broken *emotions* of your hurting wife. You will need to feel that hurt. You will need to be pierced with the swords of emotional agony that have caused your wife to bleed and perhaps to emotionally die. I'm certain that I don't have the words to adequately dredge the depths or cross the expanse of that kind of pain. I can only give you a glimpse of what I understand.

I believe it's safe to say that every woman wants to be cherished. She wants to be the jewel of her husband's eye. She wants to be desired by him. She wants to be loved regardless of her appearance, her talents, her energy, or any other outward quality. She wants to be loved because she is in your heart. She wants to be so completely entwined in everything that you are that you can't help but notice her in everything you do or think. I'm not speaking of her acting clingy, self-absorbed, or needy in a weak way. I'm talking about her desire to truly share a life with you. She wants to be one cloth with you, so to speak, in the most profound way. This desire is so much a part of her being that she will suffer greatly if she doesn't sense that this is happening at some level.

My wife never felt connected to me in this way. She said she felt that I would be better off without her, that she was in the way, and that she didn't feel she was good enough. In short, she felt like she had no value whatsoever to me. There was a constant buzz in her brain that said, *My husband doesn't care what happens to me.* Several times toward the end of our marriage, she confessed that she didn't care either. No woman should ever have to say these things to the man who is supposed to love her as Christ loves the church.

And all this time, amazingly, I thought that our relationship was pretty good. That may sound cruel to you—that I didn't notice the level of pain my wife was experiencing. It's not, though, once you understand that I was feeling as much as I had the ability to feel. My ability was simply not very great. At the same time my wife was feeling those awful things, I was actually feeling closer to her than I had felt to anyone ever in my life. She was loving, nurturing, and fun. I loved her. I cared about her. I provided for her. I thought about her all the time. I showed her that I was thinking about her by paying attention to her needs, sending her cards if I had to travel, bringing things home for her that she liked, staying in constant contact if I was away, and a hundred other things that I thought told her that I loved her. I really did think I was showing her my love. That was the big disconnect—she was suffering while I thought everything was right as rain.

Until the day we met with our marriage counselor. That conversation is forever seared in my mind. We were talking about how my wife felt in our relationship. She was hurting and angry, but she wasn't trying to hurt me. She was never like that. Our counselor asked her, "How does a woman feel when her husband is incapable of emotional connection?"

She answered, "Like a whore!"

Her words ripped through me like a lava-hot bullet.

I don't know anything a gentle Christian woman could say about her marriage that would be more damning. What she meant by it was this: *In the absence of intimate emotional connection, sexual contact makes a woman feel filthy.*

My inability to emotionally weave my life together with hers told her implicitly that she was no better than a prostitute. Intimacy in marriage is all about fulfilled relationship—not merely about physical pleasure.

May I make a side note here to the men? Pornography, whether it's through media or in your mind, is pleasure without intimacy. It is pleasure without relationship, and if it's part of your life, *kill it.* You will make no progress toward your wife or your Lord. If your intimate relationship with your wife is not fulfilling to you, it is probably because she is not feeling connected to you (and you to her) in the more important areas of your marriage. Concentrate on your inner man, and the outer man will find fulfillment.

The revelation about how intimacy felt to my wife was just one of many things that made me cringe as we tried to work through her frayed sensitivities. I say *cringe* in the sense that it made me hurt in ways I had never hurt before. I did not want to be the man who did that damage. I hadn't thought I *could* do that kind of damage. I wanted to be someone else. I wanted to be the man who could meet the needs of my wife's heart. I was so ashamed of myself for my inability to see what I was doing before it was too late.

That's another motivation for this book. I want everyone who touches this book to see what they desperately need to see. Don't let one more second slip into eternity until you've scrutinized yourself and your relationships in this light.

I was too late, and I knew it as I sat through several sessions of marriage counseling and subsequent conversation. I felt the impending doom. I knew with each new revelation that I had killed my wife's heart. My friend Matt, whom you'll meet in another chapter, said something to me then that applies here: A woman's heart closes a little at a time, and once shut it is almost impossible to reopen. I can regretfully attest to that. I spent many days and nights weeping over the pain I had caused, the loss we were experiencing, the unsure future, and the utter failure of half of my life, perhaps my entire life to that point. When God opens a wound like this, He is the only one who can heal it. I wept often and cried out to Him more and learned to trust Him completely. I had no reserve for this kind of pain, nothing to draw on. I had to feel this one utterly.

Perhaps the most tragic part of this pain was that it mirrored all the ways my wife said she was hurting. I was going through every compressed emotion that she had been feeling for years. My thoughts and my tears often reminded me of things she had said and ways she felt. It was as if God wanted me to truly hurt in every way she had. He wanted me never to forget it. I think I have some insight into why David chose to be punished by three days of God's wrath in 1 Chronicles 21 (ESV) rather than be given over to the hand of man. David said in verse 13, "I am in great distress. Let me fall into the hand of the LORD, for His mercy is very great, but do not let me fall into the hand of man." God wounded me, but He also had mercy to deliver me.

I could give many more examples of how my disconnection affected my wife, but I don't want to belabor something that I think already hits home. If this affects you, I'm guessing that you are fairly relational and are reading this to understand, perhaps to find some answers to, a man in your life who is disconnected. I hope you find some healing here. If this sounds like a lot of hyperemotional tripe to you, then you may be the disconnected guy who shuns emotion, thinks he's connected, and thinks the market is already too flooded with relationship "psychobabble" and "how to love your wife" stuff. My hope is that very few fit this description. I hope that most people who read this will take it seriously, making a close examination of their marriage or heading-toward-marriage relationship and seeking the Lord for any adjustments that are needed.

My suggestion to make a close examination will in many cases, sadly, fall on deaf ears. It's not that we don't want to hear, but rather that the disconnected man (like I was) truly *can't* hear.

So how did I hear? What was it that revealed my disconnection? How did I go from being a disconnected man to becoming a connected, relational man?

Chapter 3

How Will He Ever Know?

Having coffee with a friend is not supposed to turn into a personal crisis, but it did for me.

I don't remember what the weather was like outside the café that day, but I remember the weather change in my heart. My friend Matt was completely unaware that our conversation and his candid observation would be the rocks that the fragile ship of my heart was about to break upon. I arrived for our meeting sporting my normal sunny disposition. I ordered my coffee and sat down. After a quick hello, Matt said, "Jim, I have something I want to say to you—something that I don't think you will like, but something you need to hear and to understand."

"Sure! I'm interested to hear what you have to say," I said.

"Do you realize that you don't care about me at all?" he said. "I do not matter to you one bit. Relationally, I am irrelevant to you. Don't get me wrong...you'd help me if I needed help, but let's be clear...you'd help me in the same way you'd help a perfect stranger. That's not the same as caring about me and valuing me as a friend."

I mildly protested, "I like you. We're sitting here having coffee together, aren't we?" I smiled, giving a nervous chuckle, and thought, *Where is he going with this?*

"I didn't say you didn't like me," Matt said. "I said you don't care about me, which is another way of saying you don't love me. And if you're willing to be honest with yourself, I'll prove it to you."

"Okay," I said, my smile now gone as I grew very uncomfortable with what Matt was about to unearth.

"Let's get real...when I walk out that door, you wouldn't care at all if we never spoke again. You'd carry on without another thought about me. When someone matters to you—when you actually love another person—that could never happen. Now, look me in the eye and tell me I'm wrong."

I paused, wanting to answer differently but knowing I couldn't. "It's true," I finally said. "I'd carry on without another thought of you. I've always been able to do that."

"And the real problem is that you think this is normal!" Matt said. "It doesn't even occur to you that there is anything wrong with this. But there is something deeply wrong, because this kind of thinking, this kind of living, it's twisted, it's broken, and it's completely the opposite of how we are instructed in the Bible to live."

Matt then showed me the verse in 1 Peter 4:8 where we are instructed to love one another fervently. "It's not that you don't love me fervently, Jim," Matt said. "You don't love me at all. I'm guessing that something occurred when you were young, something that caused you to decide that the price of caring about another person was too high to pay. So, you smiled, went along, and protected yourself by never allowing anyone to matter to you. You've been hiding in the open ever since. Deep inside you there's something broken, Jim. I'm confident that God wants you to discover what it is so He can touch that place with His healing hand and teach you how to love another person."

I found myself sputtering a weak agreement.

All the while I was acknowledging the truth of his observation, I was fighting inside, trying to convince myself that I didn't want to be the man my friend had just described. But I *was* that man.

Imagine skipping through life having almost nothing bother you deeply or break your rhythm. Picture constant lightheartedness, fun, nonchalant happiness, carefree joy, and a resiliently healthy temperament. That was me—at least as far as I was willing to examine myself. Until my friend spoke truth to my heart.

I spent the next few days after my talk with Matt in a profound haze. I was disoriented, wandering through the pathways of my mind, searching for lost pieces of the puzzle of my life. I kept asking over and over, *What is wrong with me? How can I be any different than who I am? Why am I here and how did I get here? How can a simple question lead to such inner pain? Why do I suddenly feel so lonely?* And similar other questions, only to be met with a thick feeling of nothing. My friend's words left me hollow and broken. I despised the man I was discovering inside, but I didn't know how to be different.

One of the few comforts I experienced in those days was some wisdom shared by Sy Rogers in a teaching I had listened to several times in the past. His advice: "We don't ever need to go rummaging in the past to discover what shadows lie there. When God is ready to deal with our shadows (and by deduction, when we are ready), He will bring them to the forefront." I took comfort in the fact that God must be in control of the situation, because I certainly hadn't asked for this.

I don't know if you've ever experienced a tectonic shift, the opening of a gaping hole in your life that draws you into its abyss. I did that day. I can't describe the shadow that settled over me except to say that it was tactile. I could feel it in every atom of my being. I could sense it with every thought. It chafed against every nuance of my besieged emotions. I suppose I'm still struggling with it, or against it, as the case may be.

This tectonic life shift led me through corridors of doubt, numb wanderings, anger, despair, and emptiness, but never denial. I knew all too well the certainty of the accusation, even though Matt never intended to hurt me with his remark. In those dark hallways of my mind I found myself alone, over and over again. I was alone with my heart, and my heart was encased in some sort of impenetrable armor. I pounded and pounded on it but it didn't give way. "What is wrong with me!" I heard myself repeat in silent despair.

I remember telling myself, "I have to *feel* this," even as a nagging hopelessness drove me to doubt that I ever could feel it. I had spent most of my life in a vaguely emotionless blur. I remember very few deeply emotional events or relational connections. The ones I do remember left me in such a blubbering, utterly simpering state that I dismissed them immediately. I didn't like that condition. So I guess I learned to avoid those memories, and I think each time I did I painted another coat of lacquer on my heart. I unplugged. I disengaged. I turned away. I self-protected. I detached. I disconnected.

This was my pain, but there was a lot of pain being spread around in those days. Pain that was unfortunately shared by those who loved me dearly but had no clue how to help me. For those in a relationship with a disconnected man, there is pain, often unspoken, often deeply damaging, but always very real. If you are feeling that pain, then I encourage you to read on. You may find some help in the chapters to come.

Chapter 4

Getting Sucked into the Vacuum

Do you suspect (or know) that your partner is disconnected? Have your attempts to connect left you feeling like you've gotten too close to a black hole, that you've lost some of your light? Is it a drain to even think about trying again? Do you feel important to your spouse? Does he make you feel precious? Does he make you feel cherished?

If you care about your relationship and you love your mate, then you are probably still trying. When you do, you may feel like a fly desperately trying to escape the suction of a vacuum cleaner. The overpowering draw of your desire to connect pulls you, and you know it will kill you if you keep going there. You keep hoping for a different outcome, only to be disappointed.

The emotional trauma you may be experiencing with your

disconnected man can take several forms, some of them listed below. A good way to begin to move toward healing and healthy relationship is to explore and understand your current feelings. There may be no way to cover the gamut of emotions you are feeling or have felt or will feel in the midst of your relationship, but let's uncover as many as we can and discuss how they can affect you. If you can connect with your own emotions, then you will be on much better footing to try to help him connect with you.

LONELY

You may feel lonely in a relationship with a disconnected man. Your desire for a real conversation, for his eyes to look back at you with understanding, or for a knowing tenderness may often be met with empty activity or a sort of numb ignorance. He will try to serve you or give you something or work harder, but he won't truly connect in the way you need. You ache for a sign, a longing gaze, a truly emotional conversation, a tender touch that shows that you are in his heart. When it doesn't happen, that overwhelming wave of loneliness crashes onto your emotional shore, nearly drowning you.

But remember, it doesn't have to stay this way. Beware that loneliness can be a place of great temptation. Don't give in to it. Instead use the lonely times to pray and plan for how God will bring about connection in times to come. Keep dreaming and trusting God to do His work. Later on in this book you'll find practical suggestions on how to help your man connect with you.

Remember: He probably doesn't feel lonely. In fact, he may feel more connected to you than he's ever felt to anyone. He probably truly loves and appreciates you. He just doesn't have the inner tools yet to show you. I loved and appreciated my wife. She was the only one I shared personal things with. The "emotional" things I really couldn't describe well in the rare times they came to my mind. I depended on her to be there. I didn't need much emotional support, but I needed her.

Your man needs you. So pray for him. He also needs those inner tools even more than you need him to have them. God wants him to have them too. Join hands with God in this endeavor and wait patiently on the Lord. He wants to do as much in your heart as He does in your mate's.

EMPTY

Loneliness pours itself into emptiness. But loneliness and hopelessness are the fruit of your mind, not your God-empowered spirit. You may feel that every time you beat this feeling down and move out of its grasp it somehow circles back around to attack with a new vengeance. Your mate's distance doesn't help. You may be crying out inside, *If I could only reach out to him and help him see!*

Dear sister, you are filled with all the fullness of God (Ephesians 3:19). He can fill all the empty places. I don't know exactly how He does it, but He does. He will meet you in your tears. He will comfort you and wrap you in His arms. Wait on Him, pursue Him, be found by Him. He will carry you through the empty times.

UNNEEDED

Do not listen to the voices that whisper, *You are not needed.* No one needs you more than the disconnected man you are paired with. Especially now that you're learning the truth about his situation and what he needs. You are his best chance for intimacy and relationship in this world. He may not know it, but it's absolutely the case. Fight this lie of being unneeded with all your might.

Please listen to me here if you are married to this man. God has joined you together in the deepest, most real, and yet mystical way. He didn't make a mistake when uniting the two of you. You were put together to help and refine one another. You have the keys to this man's heart, even if it seems that you can't find his heart. He desperately needs you to stay with him and look for the opportunities to use those keys. Again, he probably doesn't know what he needs, but God does. And He will guide you. There is no one better or more deserving than you to be there when the door to his heart swings open.

ANXIOUS

Anxiety is another word for fear. Of course you're afraid. You're afraid that he'll never change. You're afraid that all your dreams of being his beautiful princess are gone. You're afraid that you'll really never feel loved. You fear that his disconnection means that he's looking elsewhere. You fear your heart dying. You fear that your children will be similarly handicapped. You fear a future of trying to get a response, with no response. The list could go on.

What do you do with fear?

The Bible says, "Fear not!" approximately 140 times. Jesus said it more than anyone else. God understands that you fear. Your fear doesn't anger Him—He has mercy. I encourage you to look up all the times the Bible says, "Fear not!" and revel in them. Get in the habit of submitting every fear to God. Take each one of them to Him as soon as you feel it creeping in.

FRUSTRATION

Of course you're frustrated. You married or started a relationship with this man in order to love and be loved. Your dreams for closeness and mutual life may seem like a vapor now. You wanted a whole man, a man who would enfold you in his arms, initiate love, cherish you, and be there through good and bad. When that doesn't happen, it's completely normal to be frustrated and hurt. So, don't beat yourself up.

However, saying, "It's completely normal" does not mean it's acceptable to stay frustrated. Nursing your frustration will only lead to bitterness. Through the power of the Holy Spirit, you must overcome the frustration. Don't try to do this on your own. Don't isolate yourself. Fighting the battle against frustration is something you need help with. Do you have a Christian sister or spiritual leader you can confide in and ask to pray for you and keep you accountable? If so, don't delay. If not, pray for one—God will provide.

BITTER

This is a tough one. We don't always know when we've crossed the line from frustration to bitterness. The bitterness could be with your mate or your Master, but if it exists, you need to take quick action. How do you know if you've crossed the line? The Bible calls bitterness a root (Hebrews 12:15). What do roots do if left in the ground? They continue to grow. If you pick a weed but leave the root, a new weed will grow in its place, oftentimes hardier than the one you picked. The new plant is just like the old one. That's how you know it's bitterness—it's not different each time, like a momentary frustration, but rather it's the same aggravation.

If your frustration has turned to bitterness, it will bear the fruit of bitterness. Whatever it looks like for you to express frustration, you will find it coming back unbidden. It will express itself in times that don't make sense and perhaps in ways that are unusual. It's a persistent energy that hums in the background. I discovered this when I realized I could go for months, even years, without a blowup and then suddenly explode about the messy house I had been living in without complaint for all that time. Maybe I tripped over something I left on the floor because there was no place on the table to put it. So I blamed my frustration on the mess (and by extension, the mess makers) instead of my own failure to find a place for what I just tripped over.

The slightest provocation can sometimes create a burst of impatience or anger. If this describes you, then you may have a stubborn root of bitterness lying agitated under the surface of your life. It's time to pull it up—no matter how deep it is. You may find that you need help with this. Our hearts are deceptive and we can't always see for ourselves what is plain to others. Seek out wise counsel for this one. Be aggressive, though: Roots of bitterness are relentless and they will hurt many of the people around you if you don't eradicate them.

UNLOVED

I am so sorry that you are feeling this way. It's true that a disconnected man has a great deal of trouble making you feel loved. He doesn't have a great need to feel loved or—perhaps more accurately—it takes very little to make him feel loved. The fact that you are still with him probably satisfies him. His fulfillment comes from other directions—not that it should; it just does for now. Again, this can all change!

We were all created to love and be loved. Our souls crave it. We die without it. God pours it out in abundance. If you are depending upon your disconnected mate to fill your love-starved heart, then you may be in a bad way. No one can give you what God alone has reserved for Himself. God is the initiator of love. He will allow no one to usurp His place in your heart or to substitute a temporary love for His eternal *agape*! Even marriage is temporary. It was only meant to last while we live on this earth. We have eternity to live out. If there is no marriage in heaven and no mates, who will love us? God will and does. God desires to fill you up with His overwhelming love. Paul prayed in Ephesians 3:18 that "you may have strength to comprehend with all the saints what is the breadth and length and height and depth, and to know the love of Christ that surpasses knowledge." Spend your time drawing near to God, and He has promised that He will draw near to you.

DISCOURAGEMENT

Discouragement is the natural outcome of the feelings above. It is a constant drain to repeatedly try to get some sort of response that meets your emotional need. It depletes you in ways you may not be able to express. Discouragement and perhaps depression follow. Let me point you back to your loving Savior. I may sound like a one-note symphony here, but it's a very sweet note. Jesus is your true lover. He is your helper and strong tower. His arms are big enough to hold all of your disappointments, and His hand is gentle enough to wipe away all your tears. Return to Him over and over and over.

DIRTY

I referred to this in the last chapter about your sexual relationship with your husband. Has sexual contact made you feel filthy, as my ex-wife described? If so, I want to validate your feeling while at the same time giving you some insight that I hope will help you. Your husband has no idea that you feel this way, unless you've told him. If you've told him, it's most likely something he truly can't process. He has no ability to entertain such a thought. *He* feels connected—as much as a man with stunted relational abilities *can*. He is probably thinking that everything in your marriage is normal and good, and if he heard that you feel dirty, it would be shocking to him, even incomprehensible.

★ ★ ★

So how do you manage these feelings?

First of all, own them. They are not evil. Your heart and soul know that love is supposed to be all-encompassing, and sexual fulfillment blossoms from the tender everyday attentions your mate should be showing you. When these are absent, your inclination is to feel used. Take those feelings to Jesus too. Let Him apply the proper balm for your healing. Then please hear me again: Your mate probably doesn't have a clue that he comes across this way. He is trying to love you. He's broken inside, and he can't express love in exactly the way you will best receive it. Keep reading, because you'll find help to bring him around. These are deep issues that require deep healing, so I want to ask, "Are you in it for the long haul?" Are you completely committed to God's way of doing things? Will you work and wait for Him to change your husband? If so, then take heart. It's going to get better.

The recurring themes in my admonitions are to trust God and be patient. I know these are the two most difficult disciplines that we are asked to do. We don't like to wait, and it's hard to trust the God we cannot see. I can tell you that God doesn't want your man to be nonrelational, and He is more passionate than you are about it. He also doesn't want you to miss out on what He can do with your mate. His heart and His power, tempered by His patience and grace, are bent on making your man like Jesus. And Jesus is the very essence of love. His is the originator of affection (1 John 4:8). He is the fountain of every good thing that comes from love. He is the bastion of your heart and He wants your husband to be such a harbor for you. He is busy at work in that chamber of affection behind the stone walls of your man's exterior. He works from the inside out—but His work always gets done.

Hold on to these assurances. They are real. God can be trusted. He will renovate the broken places in your man's life. How He'll do it and exactly how long it will take is yet to be seen. If your man is a reader, then maybe he'll read this with you and take some steps. If not, then you will have to trust God to enable you to win him over with your godly, loving behavior. Either way, God is not content to leave him where he is. God wants your man to be a relational man. The next chapter will help him to see his relational inabilities in language he can understand.

Chapter 5

Walls You Can't See

Brother, are you ready to see yourself? I'm addressing this chapter to you. From a formerly disconnected man to a yet-to-discover-his-disconnectedness man, I want to invite you to get very serious for a few minutes. I don't know how this book found its way into your hands, but it doesn't matter. Let's take it as God's providence in your life.

If these things apply to you, it is probably a mystery to you that they do. Let's try to unlock that mystery a bit. The first question I want to ask you is, "Are you a disconnected man?"

Perhaps the best way to approach this is to ask a series of questions. Will you answer honestly?

- Do you now or have you ever felt deeply intertwined with anyone, in the sense that you really couldn't live without them?

- Do a lot of people consider you to be very competent at what you do?
- Have you been a natural overachiever most of your life? In other words, has success come easily, almost effortlessly, to you?
- Do you have fond memories of tender moments with your parents?
- Did you have a lot of dating relationships and breakups before you found your wife?
- How long did it typically take to recover from a breakup?
- Have you ever had a very close friend or family member die? What was their name?
- How long did you grieve?
- Do you feel a hole in your heart where they used to be?
- Do you spend much time reminiscing about the past, or do you usually move on and look to the future?
- Do overtly emotional movies or stories deeply affect you?
- What was happening the last time you broke down emotionally and cried?
- Does change bother you?
- Are you able to walk away from friends without staying in touch?
- Do you ever truly miss anyone? Is it a rare feeling to miss someone? I'm not asking if you ever feel lonely—I'm asking if you miss a special person.
- Is it easy for you to leave a job and move on to another?
- Are you passionate about your wife?
- Does your love for your wife overcome you sometimes?

- Has anyone told you they thought you were proud (or arrogant)?
- If you have children, is it hard to leave them when you have to be away?
- Do you get irrationally angry from time to time?
- Describe the relationship you've had with your mom and dad.
- Describe the relationship with your wife from YOUR perspective.
- Describe your relationship with your wife from HER perspective.
- Do you find it a bit irritating to answer these questions and think in this way?

I'm not a psychiatrist. I'm not even a good counselor. I'm just a guy who spent most of his life as a relationally disconnected man. The questions I'm asking are the questions that helped me understand who I was and why I was hurting people.

When I asked myself these questions, I didn't like the guy I found answering them. God used these and other things to wring me out, renovate me, and restore me. So let's spend some time discussing your answers. What I say here may be relevant to you or not, but I dare you to take your answers directly to the Holy Spirit and ask them of Him one by one. Ask Him to reveal those things you've believed that aren't true, and then let Him tell you the truth about yourself. We humans are expert liars when it comes to self-examination. The Spirit, though, is an expert at revelation!

First up, what about your competence? I had a friend call me omni-competent once. I'm very capable of managing many things, doing them well, and leaving things better than I found them. I'm also capable of completely walking away from my accomplishments and not really thinking about them again. I move on quickly. Once in a while I'll think, *I did good there!*

One very important thing about my competence is that it was always with tasks, organization, skills, or managing outcomes. It was never relational. I was not competent at creating and maintaining relationships. I had lots of friends and usually had a great time with them, but I had no lasting, close friendships. I didn't connect strongly with people, and once they passed out of my radar range, I really didn't try to keep in contact.

Would you identify yourself like that? Are you really good at what you do? Do you look forward to the next thing, do it well, and then move on? I know this sounds like a description of a great employee, but it can also be a symptom of a problem, if all your success is task-oriented and nonrelational. Do you ever *miss* the emotional connection you had with the people you've interacted with? If not, take it as an indication that you have at least a little disconnectedness going on. If you don't miss it, it was probably never there.

How did you answer the mom and dad questions? How about the dating ones, and the death of a loved one? Is this sounding too much like a Freudian interrogation or a self-help analysis? Hang with me, we're going somewhere with it.

In the past, my idea of love was twofold: *recognition after achievement* and *being provided for.* My idea of love was not long conversations about how someone felt, or hugs, or snuggling, or knowing what someone in the family was struggling with.

Love was unspoken, and touch was unknown. I remember many times hearing my family talk about a tragedy or joy in someone's life and I would respond, "I didn't know about that," only to have them tell me they had been talking about it for weeks (or longer) and wondered how I could have missed it. I missed it because I wasn't interested in people. I missed a lot of important things that way.

Having grown up this way didn't make me continue that way, though. I became a hugger and a husband who said *I love you* a lot. As far as I knew, I was miles ahead of where my family ever was and where I had been within my family. But outward displays of affection are not enough. I was displaying what I thought was love, but I wasn't feeling intimately connected to anyone. *Connection is the feeling that someone else is a part of you and you are part of them.* Losing them would cause you to feel incomplete, devastatingly partial, and deficient. Do you feel that way about anyone? I wasn't capable of losing a part of myself if a friend or loved one died. In fact, I did lose my dad. I loved my dad in the way that I described our family loved, but I didn't really know my dad. We weren't close. We weren't connected. I respected him and enjoyed his company, but we never had a serious heart-to-heart talk. Never. When he died, I grieved for a short while but I never felt like a part of me was missing.

I remember missing my wife and my kids from time to time, but it didn't hurt. And I missed them only intermittently. I was so focused on what was in front of me that everything else was pushed out. That in itself was a warning sign, but I couldn't see it.

Do you think much about the past in order to remember it? Do you like change and have little problem adapting to new jobs, houses, or people? Do you really feel connected to anything? Are you a little proud of your ability to handle change? Do you have friends with whom you've kept in contact for years? Do you talk about more than just the weather, the kids, or last night's game? Have any of your friends joked that you could walk out the door and never miss them? Or maybe you already have walked out the door and not missed them. All of these questions are meant to dig into your soul and disturb you if you are disconnected. Each of these questions may also describe a normal and temporary disconnectedness that many people feel from time to time. What I am referring to, however, is a habitual state of being.

Furthermore, if you can name the best friends you've had and then find that it's been a long time since you contacted them or had a serious conversation with them, then you may not have really connected with them. If you have to be reminded every time a "good" friend's name comes up that they had a tragedy occur, or what their kid's names are, or that they are divorced, or any such intimate details, then you probably aren't really connected. The emotional details of their lives aren't sinking deeply into your heart, so you forget them.

Similarly, do you have difficulty recalling the last deeply emotional conversation you had with someone—not when they were emotional, but when *you* felt deep emotion? Was it real? I struggled the most to feel what other people were feeling. If they were relating a tragedy to me, I usually didn't try to imagine myself in their shoes. Even when I did, I don't think I really *felt* the tragedy. I could grasp it intellectually, but I didn't get emotionally involved. I wasn't a good comforter. I wasn't the guy you would go to for sympathy and understanding. I could give you the Bible solution to your grief but I couldn't empathize with your pain. I think it hindered my prayers for others as well. Since I wasn't able to identify with them and feel their pain or praise, I really couldn't pray accurately for them. I pray more effectively now for others because I feel true joy and pain.

The topics above are relatively easy. Let's move on to the hard stuff. What about your wife? Did you have trouble describing your marriage from *her* perspective? If you wrote it down and gave it to her, would she honestly say that it represented the condition of her heart? Do you know the condition of her heart? Not knowing the condition of my wife's heart led to the greatest personal tragedy I've ever experienced. My wife told me she never felt loved by me and she wouldn't continue to try to be loved by me. She was done. You've probably never considered that to be a risk. I never did. But there it was, her departure screaming at me every day, crushing me over and over again. It was the only thing that ever got through and broke down the wall around my heart. And I could finally see what she had felt for many years. I can't blame her for doing what she thought was necessary to preserve her heart and give it a chance to live again.

I believe you are reading this because God wants to give you a chance to avoid what I experienced. You may still have an opportunity to recognize yourself and your disconnection, and make an "about-face" before it's too late. Take the test— write down the description of your marriage from your wife's perspective. Then give it to your wife, and ask her to read it and give you *honest* feedback. It just might be the first step you'll take to truly hear her heart. Please do this. I promise that God will cover for you. He is faithful. Cast your anxiety and fear on Him and let the healing begin!

If anything in this chapter applies to you and reveals disconnectedness in your relationships, I can tell you without any reservation that you are disconnected from God as well. It doesn't matter if you are a pastor preaching every week and serving a flock (I was), a business owner who has a company to care for (I was), a father who is loving his children to the best of his ability (I was), or a husband thinking that he's loving his wife (I was). If the Holy Spirit is showing you that you are disconnected in any of the ways we've described, then you are also struggling with your relationship to God. A man cannot be disconnected from God's people and be connected with God. Just read 1 John and you'll see what I mean. (Note: For further discussion of the realities and challenges I imagine these questions might have revealed, see the Appendix, "What Do the Questions in Chapter 5 Reveal?" at the end of this book.)

I believe that a significant part of the Western male population is disconnected. Some worse than others, but nonetheless many need improvement. If you picked up this book simply to skim it and now find yourself here, I encourage you to keep reading. If the content doesn't apply directly to you, it may apply to many of your friends, and you can help them. If part or all of it applies to you, then please read it all—it might just save your life, because your life *consists* of your relationships!

I indicated before that human relationships (especially with Christian brothers) often reveal the health of our relationship with God—they are a barometer of our real spiritual heart-ties to our Heavenly Father. Marriages are even more so. Marriages to disconnected men often challenge this concept. A disconnected man truly feels connected to his wife and to his God, but someone looking on from the outside may find that statement to be unbelievable. They see his distance even though he doesn't.

What is a wife to do with a man like that? She *knows* he's disconnected. She feels his disconnection. She cries herself to sleep when he's gone. Her eyes search for her reflection in his, only to find an abyss of disappointment. She's desperate to be loved. She aches to truly know him and for him to know her. Her heart breaks little by little, closes inch by inch, until at last it shuts tight...and locks. She could never get into his heart and now she can't take the chance of letting him into hers. Please don't lock the door. Read on and find some hope.

Brother, if you just read what I wrote without emotion, you are in trouble. If you can imagine your bride's heart breaking, her soul shutting down, without feeling a pang of guilt, then your future path is fraught with peril. If you felt some pain but were unaware that your wife might be feeling like that, then the next chapter is for you. A bride needs to know she is loved and valued, and a husband needs to show it. Let's explore how that happens.

Chapter 6

Disconnected Love

Two questions often take up residence in the back of a disconnected couple's mind. The wife asks, "Does my disconnected man love me?" The husband asks, "How can she not know that I love her?"

God created everyone to ask the question "Am I loved?" (John 13:34–45). Our hearts yearn for the answer to be yes. You've been begging for an answer, searching for evidence, maybe even shouting and fighting for some sort of affectionate attention. You may be the type who stuffs the desire deep inside, where it gnaws at your sanity. You would do anything for the lasting assurance that your man truly, deeply loves you.

Hearing that he loves you may go against everything you feel. It fights against your experience. You probably don't feel loved. You may have a couple of memories where a mist of affection passed over your thirsty heart, but it's never been a running stream, let alone a waterfall. Will you take it on faith from a formerly disconnected man when I tell you without reservation that your disconnected man loves you? And that *you* have the power to help him learn how to show it? You read that right. You, dear sister, have the power to unlock your man's heart in such a way that the proof of his love will flow freely through the emotional desert of your heart.

I would give anything to have told my wife what I just told you. I didn't know how, though, and neither does your man. But I want you to hear this—your sweet, eternal Father made that man with an eternal capacity for love. He gave him the Spirit of love when He saved your husband. He desires more than anything to love you through him. He will ceaselessly pursue this man's heart in an effort to breach its doors and topple its ramparts. God will destroy every high thing that prevents love from escaping your good man's heart. As for your man, somewhere far beyond the borders of his heart lies an oasis of love yet to be discovered. He's never seen the border, let alone ventured past it. He needs a guide.

How can I say that I'm confident he loves you, when you could tell me in no uncertain terms that he doesn't? That's the second part of this disconnected equation. I can also say with confidence that he doesn't have the equipment to prove his love to you. As tragic as that sounds, both for you and for him, it doesn't have to be a permanent condition.

It may help you to know a little about how he missed the sign-up for relational equipment and perhaps how you missed his disconnection before you married him.

It may not be entirely accurate to say that your man didn't get the emotional equipment for connectedness, since God gives relational tools to everyone. It's more like this: Think of a piece of equipment you've seen but have no idea how to use. You may not even know what its use is. For instance, do you know what an atmospheric pressure ionization mass spectrometer is? I don't, and if you do, I'm impressed. If I saw one, I wouldn't know what it did, how to use it, or even how to turn it on. What's more, I probably wouldn't care. Suppose someone gave me one. Suppose they had it delivered with no warning, no instructions, no return address, and no indication whatsoever as to why I have it or what to do with it. What am I likely to do with it? I can tell you that if it's small enough to put on a shelf and forget about, I'm taking that path. And if it's too large to fit through my front door, then it will sit on my doorstep for eternity. I don't have time to be bothered with stuff I don't understand and can't use.

And that's the brutal point. The equipment was delivered, but no one ever showed your disconnected man how to use it at the time he was most ready to learn. It's on a shelf somewhere, behind those walls that he doesn't know are there, in a place he's never visited. He doesn't have the time or the motivation to go exploring for something he's not likely to understand or be able to use. It's immeasurably discouraging for him to even think about it.

Expecting your man to be relational may be a mistake. You will have to teach him how to be relational.

Ladies, I want to invite you to adopt a new perspective. Up till now, you've assumed that your man is relational and he's just not paying attention to you, that he's neglecting you. I don't believe that's true. I want to invite you to stop expecting him to be relational and see that you will need to show him how. You have to teach him how to use the equipment God gave him— the equipment without instructions that's shoved into a dark corner in a back room of his emotional makeup.

Your man doesn't know he has access to the piece of equipment that could change everything; it could mend the deep, old relational wounds. But if he knew it would cost him every last trace of who he knows himself to be to get to it and learn how to use it, would he do it? I can tell you that if you had mentioned something like this to me before God put His finger on my need, I would have dismissed it. I didn't think I needed anything of the sort. So these questions, these points of realization, must be perfectly timed in concert with the Holy Spirit. Further, if he knew that he had to become someone completely different from who he is, if he had to watch every cell of his emotional makeup explode in searing heart-pain, could he muster the courage to do it? If you told him that the building of his soul has to be completely ripped down to the dust beneath the foundation, could he possibly say yes? This is what he's up against. You have to realize what you are asking. Realize also that you are worth it and that God is asking with you.

The piece of equipment we are talking about, and that he truly needs, won't cure all wounds but it will cure the aching of your heart. And if he's a good man, he will endure the hell of his disconnected heart to get to it, learn it, and eventually become an expert in its use. In truth, he is probably willing to suffer untold waves of agony for you if he only knew you needed him to. Therein lies the challenge. How can you let him know this without crushing him or being crushed yourself? We will tackle that question later, but for now, he's wondering how it can be possible that you can't see how much he loves you.

The disconnected man is a loving man. Granted, there may be a spectrum of disconnection that needs to be considered, but on the whole, a disconnected man is capable of love. We are created in God's image and God is love, so we know this man is capable. I know that I loved my wife, my children, my parents, my congregation, and my friends as a disconnected man. It was a disconnected love, but at the same time, it was truly love. I can honestly say that it even felt like love to me, but remember that I had no practical knowledge of how to use the relational equipment it took to communicate that love. The best I knew was to do what my parents did to show love—reward performance and provide. To provide meant that I sometimes worked two or three jobs in addition to being a pastor. I did whatever I could find, taxi driver, mail carrier, explosives technician, cabinet installation, and more. I sold everything from insurance to industrial conveyors. When I was working, I assumed I was expressing love.

By *performance* I mean "meeting expectations," or in the kids' case, being obedient. Looking back, I can say I wasn't very good at positively praising my family for their accomplishments. Probably because my expectations were unreasonable. I was too hard on them and I honestly can't remember (from those disconnected days) an event where I celebrated accomplishments with them. I know there were some but I can't bring them to mind. Isn't that sad! Nevertheless, as I mentioned before, I even added a healthy dose of hugs and verbal *I love yous* to the mix.

That's what made things such a mystery to me. I was doing everything my parents did, as well as what I had seen other loving families do. The issue was that *doing* wasn't *being*. I was doing all the right things but without an inner connection that made them real to others. So, I did more of what I was doing, with more energy and more desire, without ever detecting that I was coming up empty. I don't remember ever getting even a subtle inner message that my actions weren't being interpreted as love. I think my kids, and especially my wife, tried hard to tell me or show me but I was too blind to see it. Nothing penetrated. Since my wife was unable to communicate the lack in a way I could see it, there was no way I could ever have fixed it.

When the truth finally came out that my wife didn't feel loved by me, I was dazed. I had no idea how to react. I'm sure my inability to respond made it look even more as if it were true. How could I defend myself about a feeling I'd never truly experienced? I was lost. I argued and explained and showed my frustration—all the things (I was to learn later) that can drive someone further away instead of inviting them back in. I knew that I loved my wife, but all my debate turned to dust in her eyes. It was an irritant and a blinding force. She had already become exhausted trying to break through my emotional walls, and now I was becoming exhausted trying to prove I was open and had *no* walls. *How could she not know that I loved her?* was the question I didn't find an answer to in time.

If you are the man reading this, you are asking the same question in some form. You are a good man. You provide. You talk.

You give. You hug. You lead. You love. What's missing that she's not seeing? That's the mystery that you have to solve. There is something preventing her having full access to your heart.

Women have an uncanny ability to detect emotional barriers, and they hate them.

Women want in. God promised them that they could get in because they are the bride—like His church. God opens His heart to His bride. He writes her love letters. He gazes into her eyes. He dances with her. He draws her near. He sings for her and over her. He interweaves Himself inextricably with her. He becomes one with her (John 17). She will not be satisfied until she becomes one with you.

What are you going to do about it? You could continue doggedly insisting that you love her while she wilts and drops into silence. You could get angry about her inability to see your love and tell her it's all her fault. You could ignore the whole thing, think she'll never do anything about it, and plod on. Divorce courts are full of Christian women who reluctantly and probably wrongfully give up because their men were stupid. Rightly or wrongly—it's happening every day. Or you could rise out of your lethargy and charge headlong into battle to free your heart. Fight this fight, and I can assure you that your wounds will be deadly, your pain a constant torture, and your sacrifice complete. It will cost you everything as you know it. But once you suffer and die to your old self (Ephesians 5:25), you and your bride will live and thrive.

So how do you get there—to thriving? You have to take a walk. Part of visiting the blackest part of your locked-down heart is to hear what it is doing to hers. You will have to feel her pain. You will have to linger in her injury. You will have to get drenched in her tears. You will have to experience her despair. You will have to walk in her misery. I'll show you how to do it in the next chapter. It won't be easy, but you can do it. You must do it. She is worth it. And you won't have to do it alone. Your Father is watching, and He is ready to meet you on that path.

Chapter 7

Take Her Heart on a Walk

I never got a chance to do this in my marriage. I want to be clear about what I mean here. I'm not saying that you are to take her on a walk and hear what she has to say. It's not time for that yet. I'm saying that you have to enter into her heart to be engulfed by the burning disappointment that lives there. It lives alongside the love she's always had for you, but the two are so entangled they are now indistinguishable from each other.

You have to pour yourself in much the same way as pouring creamer into coffee. The creamer feels the full heat of the coffee while being mixed inseparably with it. Eventually the creamer sweetens and smooths what could be a very rough and bitter drink, but not before both are fully blended with the other. It's the rough, bitter heat that you need to feel. It's not easy. I wasn't able to do it until my wife said things I never dreamed of hearing and put the exclamation point on them by leaving and never returning. I want to help you as much as I can so you don't have to hear these things from your wife as she's walking out the door.

If by some miracle your wife's heart could be injected into the part of your brain that feels pain, you would most likely be devastated. If by some greater miracle her broken dreams could be interwoven with your most tender emotions, you would feel pain deeper than you thought possible. It's that intense. And you've never noticed.

When she was a little girl, she danced and twirled. She giggled and picked flowers and felt beautiful. She grew and dreamed of being beautiful for you. She walked the misty corridors of her dreams in pure white light, watching and waiting for her prince to come. She thought of your strength and honor and couldn't wait to be swept into the arms of such a towering gracious man as you. She couldn't wait to be cherished by her hero.

And she was, at least for a while. You came along, wooed her with tenderness and sweet words. You showed her your strength and competency. You said all the right things to transform her dreams into reality. You could do that because you are so capable, so confident, so expert, and because love is so blind. You gave her the piece of your heart you had access to, and she anticipated more.

But you were done. You gave her all the heart you could reach.

Her anticipation turned to poison, a slow poison that kills one dream at a time. She held on while her princess dreams died one after the other. She danced; you didn't smile. She twirled; you missed it. She was pretty; you ignored her. She giggled; you frowned. She no longer felt beautiful. But you didn't even know it. (Close to the end of our relationship, my wife said she felt like she kept picking flowers and I stomped on them. I had no idea and I certainly would never have intentionally done so. But that's how she felt.)

You were busy slaying dragons and wondering why she wasn't standing at the door to congratulate you when you got home. You were moving on to the next challenge while she choked on your promises. You were dragging her into *your* dreams while setting hers aflame with your ignorance. You were leisurely crushing her. I'm using the past tense and that may be a mistake. Substitute *are* for *were* as the Holy Spirit directs.

Brother, listen! For the sake of Jesus Christ, His bride and yours, *listen* to me. I understand that you can't believe this is about you, but I'm shouting to you: Your wife's dreams of having an intimate relationship are dying at the door of your heart if you are a disconnected man! Her heart is aching to know you, but you are the only one who can let her in.

She has an immense capacity for love. She keeps throwing herself at the walls of your heart, hoping they will budge, hoping she can eventually catch a shaft of light piercing through an open crack. She's so battered from the attempts that she cannot recognize herself. She's tired and helpless. She has lain at the door weeping until she has no more tears. And you don't hear her. LISTEN!

Now try to feel the worst pain you ever felt as a boy. Was it rejection? Was it loneliness? Was it anger aimed at you? Was it loss? What made your heart shut down? She feels it to a degree you never did. You cloaked your heart in impenetrable armor so it couldn't be hurt. She didn't. She has no defenses. Her heart is open to every attack, and you were supposed to protect her. But you haven't. Worse yet (in many cases), you have become the aggressor—attacking her to keep from feeling attacked yourself. When she tries to reach you, you feel threatened. So you get loud, you defend yourself, you argue her down so you won't feel what she wants you to feel. It's true, isn't it? If you can attack or put up a strong defense, then your castle is safe and you won't have to feel the emotion. Is that what is so scary—feeling the emotion?

What I just described is one of the few things I remember clearly from my disconnected years. The topics we were discussing at those times are irrelevant, although they had to do with emotions and relationships. It could have been anything from the tone in my voice with her to how I treated one of the kids at the time. When I felt my wife pushing in, trying to connect, something deep inside felt threatened. I can't say it was a completely conscious feeling but it was there. I learned to become more intense and argue my point and turn things back on her. In effect, I blamed her for being too sensitive while I was the "normal, steady" one. Fighting against the intrusion into my emotions became a habit because, subconsciously, I didn't want to risk connecting on an emotional, relational level.

The disconnected man is disconnected because *feeling* hurts too much. We mask our emotions and guard them so we don't have to hurt. But we don't realize that every hurt we avoid pierces those nearest us. The closer they are, the more wounds they suffer. Stop blocking the emotional thrusts and let the blade pierce *your* heart, lest everyone around you die from the deflections. Feel it; absorb it; cry.

If you can start feeling her pain, then you can start healing her heart. Isn't that what Jesus did? He came to us, lived with us, felt our pain, endured separation from His Father, and sacrificed Himself to the point of death and beyond it so He could save us (Ephesians 4:9–10; Hebrews 4:15; Hebrews 12:2–3; John 1:14; Matthew 27:46). Do you want to "save" your wife? By that I mean, meet her deepest need for your affection? Do what Jesus did. Go to her, live in her heart, feel her pain, endure her separation and loneliness, sacrifice yourself for her, die for her, and connect with her. She's worth it and you are the only one who can do it.

I've beaten you up pretty badly. I don't want you to feel that your wife has no active role to play. You will not be alone in your quest to get to connection. Remember that she wants and needs you there. There are some small things she can do as you battle your demons. But first she needs to understand what love looks like to you. The next chapter will help her understand how you see the relational world.

Chapter 8

The Size of Small Things

How does a disconnected man see the relational world (if he sees it at all)?

Small things that others see as normal interactions seem very big to a disconnected man. Bonding relationally is intimate and frightening. He is most likely unaware that he is avoiding relational cues. He has some vague, remote sense that every act of relationship has the potential to get inside and touch his fragile emotions. He probably doesn't know he's guarded and unavailable because he became that way so long ago, but he knows that if anything gets close to the door of his heart, it emotionally breaks him and makes him feel out of control. He doesn't like feeling that he has no control. His emotional vulnerability may not be easy to access, but it's there, and he's aware of it someplace in his subconscious. And when it gets touched, it's shocking.

I once watched the movie *A Walk to Remember* on a getaway with my wife. It's a story about a girl who would not risk a relationship because she knew she had a terminal disease. She had a list of things she desired to do before she died, and then a boy shows up, wins her heart, and helps her fulfill all her dreams, and then she dies. I was devastated. I sobbed uncontrollably, and I hated that a movie could do that to me. It made me angry inside. I didn't want to feel emotion that strongly. Your man is probably the same.

Depending on his age and his circumstances, his emotionally protective ears could be so finely tuned that he seems nervous and agitated anytime potentially relational occasions occur on the horizon. Had I known what that movie was going to do to me, I would never have watched it. In the same way, if I suspected a situation was going to be emotional or relational on more than a surface level, I would naturally avoid it. I say *naturally* in the sense of instinctively—it was something I did because something inside me was conditioned to sense danger even if I didn't understand the sense or where it came from.

This does not mean your disconnected man has no capacity for love. His love quotient is very easy to get to and express because it's right on the surface. It's also part of the reason why he thinks everything is great between you. Love looks very different to him, though, and it's difficult, if not impossible, for him to express it in ways that seem normal and relational to you. It's part of the reason you feel unloved. He can't dig deep and feel profound emotions. But he can offer up what is close at hand.

This is the challenge for you. When you love a disconnected man, you will not get deep into his heart. If you try to, he will rebuff you, maybe even acting subconsciously. That might look like he doesn't care about your needs or that he's being secretive about something. Then you might react and make him feel guilty that he's not meeting your needs. And he wants nothing more than to meet your needs. So he reacts. And then you react, and the cycle continues. All along, you just wanted to connect, and he feels threatened by the connection. Intimacy is uncomfortable for him and can make him react in ways that hurt you. Again, this doesn't have to be a permanent condition. Understanding what love looks like to him is essential for you to be able to help him connect. Once you have a grasp on today's reality, you will be better prepared for tomorrow's challenge.

So what does love look like to a disconnected man?

Based on my own experience, I've broken the information into four sections. This compartmentalized view is limited to his interactions with *you* because I'm focusing on his relationship with you, the woman who loves him. I could go into how he sees children, extended family, friends, and others, but that's for another time. Before describing how love is compartmentalized in his heart, let me give you a broad generalization of how a disconnected man sees love: *Love is something a disconnected man does, not primarily something he feels.*

This is so very important for you to grasp! He *wants* to love, and so he tries to the best of his ability. He does feel love at times but most likely much differently than you. For instance, I didn't know what it was like to miss someone, truly *miss* them! I didn't know what it felt like to have my heart hurt from being separated. I never felt worried about anyone. I do now and so I know the difference. Recently my oldest son took his first really long solo trip—a sixteen-hour, one-way drive to Los Angeles. I felt myself worrying about him, wondering what it would be like if something happened. He's an adult, but I wanted him to text me and let me know he was all right. Emotions like these were foreign to me when I was disconnected. I can certainly feel them now.

Before now, commitment, sacrifice, service, and duty were my expressions of love. When your man exercises these traits, he feels closer to you because, in his mind and heart, he's met your need. This feels like love to him. Again, these are activities he *does* rather than deeply *feels*. If the feeling doesn't penetrate too far into his tender self, then he likes it. If the feeling goes too deep, he is liable to break down. Like me after the movie!

I did *want* to love—as long as it felt safe. I also believed that I loved. I thought I was really good at it. The descriptions below will help you understand why I thought I was good at showing love. Again, remember: To a disconnected man, love is what he *does*, not what he *feels*.

DAILY LIFE

Disconnected men are often very competent men. They do things and they do them well. In their mind, love is something that is *done*, and that makes them see themselves as very good at it. They know they can do most things well if they set their minds to it. So they go through their daily routine believing that they are being loving even as those around them are begging for a scrap of affection to fall from their high table. I assumed that handling most of the kitchen duties (cooking is something I like to do), working whatever jobs it took so my wife could stay home, staying in touch throughout the day, supporting my wife in things she wanted to do, cleaning, doing yard work, paying the bills, and making a solid commitment to Friday night dates all meant love.

I want you to know that I thought about my wife constantly. Every day, no matter what I was doing, she was constantly on my mind. I was always asking myself what I could do for her. How I could provide something she needed or bring something home she would enjoy. I thought about what she would think of something I saw. I wondered if she would like being to the places I was visiting. I kept in constant contact with her about the children, or her day or mine. In my mind, this was all love. I was doing the things I was supposed to do. To a disconnected man, doing *is* loving. It brings to mind the song "Always On My Mind." I think it has been covered countless times by different artists, Willie Nelson being the most recognizable. It could have been my theme song once I learned about my disconnection. Look it up and you'll see what I'm talking about.

If I could express anything to you, dear sister, about your man's daily routine, I want you to know that it is most likely full of *you*! His sense of duty and accomplishment is truly wrapped up in you. His pleasure in work is partly because it provides for you. His successes are only really great if you cheer for him. Everything he does has an aroma of you about it. I know it doesn't seem like that very often, so I want you to hear me—his life is intertwined with yours in every way that is important and meaningful to him. If you can trust me here, accept this, and draw it into your heart, it will help you through the hard times when you feel most disconnected from him.

CONVERSATION

As you probably know, conversation is difficult for the disconnected man. Not discourse about ideas or schedules or this person or that thing—he's probably really good at those conversations. He can talk about the great plays of the game, or the details of his last hunt or fishing spot he found, or the remodel project you both are working on. He can talk about what the kids are doing and learning, but he probably won't pick up on your frustration or sadness or joy about what's going on with them. He might hear your pain or delight but won't necessarily share it emotionally—only intellectually. He can hear all about your day and ask you questions but not be deeply affected by it. He's steady and relatively changeless in an emotional sense. If you want to have a *real* conversation with him, he will try, but will most likely leave you feeling that he doesn't get it. I'm speaking of real and tangible emotional expression that connects with you and makes you feel loved.

He will try because he knows somehow you need it but he doesn't yet have access to the equipment that would enable him to fill up your heart. You may be feeling especially vulnerable about your relationship with the Lord, or upset about your body, or the worries you have about the kids. You may be feeling a deep hesitation about your future with him and need some reassurance. He doesn't get it. He's never felt that way and can't understand. From his perspective, he made a commitment to you and the kids and there is nothing that can destroy that commitment. He works hard every day to prove it, so why would you even feel that way—it's illogical to him, and offensive. He probably won't show it because he's trying to have this conversation you need so he can show you he loves you in a way he thinks you need him to.

He's engaging in these intimate conversations from time to time but remember, he is *doing* something and not necessarily *feeling* it. That's why it leaves you feeling unfulfilled. He truly believes he is doing the right thing. He knows that you need emotional conversation (whatever that looks like to him), so he wants to offer it, because he loves you. He hears your sorrows and joys and believes he's gone deep—it feels to him as if his emotional cup is full, so he's pretty sure yours is as well.

As an aside: If you are depending solely on your man to fill your emotional cup, then you are probably struggling with loneliness, sadness, grief. You need friends. You need to knit godly friends and family into the fabric of your every day. You must have confidantes who speak truth to you of your worth:

- who can emotionally feel your hurt about the kids, or about him, or about the pressures you feel to be everything that's expected of a modern woman,
- who can reassure you that you are precious and beautiful to the Lord and your husband (even if he can't express it),
- who can make you laugh and look past today,
- who can pray with you about your burdens,

- who will simply love you for who you are with no expectations.

They have to be able to hear your woes and loneliness without sending you off searching elsewhere. They need to be friends who will point you back to God and not to temporary fixes. If you don't have family or friends like this, then run, don't walk, to your prayer closet and ask God for them right now. They will buoy you through the rough waters of having a disconnected mate.

DISPLAYS OF AFFECTION

Again, remember your man *does* things that to him speak of *love*: He doesn't necessarily feel them beyond the surface. When he buys you flowers, or brings home a special treat, or hugs you or says, "I love you," or uses his special name for you, or any other similar act, he honestly believes that he's scaled the lofty mountains of love and shouted his affection from their highest peaks.

These things, these little ways he offers affection, may not be important to you. In the end, my wife told me that they weren't important to her, at least not in comparison with what she really needed. She needed me to miss her, to be incomplete without her, to crave spending time with her. I didn't have those feelings then and so it was obvious to her that they were not there. In contrast, I now feel all of those emotions. I hate being away from my wife now; I loved being alone then. I feel like I'm blundering and tripping over everything I do now without my wife's wisdom. I made most of the decisions on my own then. I have a magnetic pull at my heart and feel incomplete when we are separated now. I felt complete and capable when I tackled things by myself then. (None of this meant that I wasn't thinking about my wife then and doing everything I knew how to meet her needs and show her love.)

Now I understand. These little things he does to show his love might even become abrasive to you, since they are not tied to an eternal, passionate feeling of the two of you being bound together. That makes it difficult for you to sincerely receive them and enjoy them for what they are—his genuine expressions of love for you. I want to encourage you to try, though. Ask God to help you see with your mate's eyes when he does something for you. Remember that to him, doing *is* loving. He does love you, and you need to know it.

Once you learn to accept his limited ability to show love, and then to appreciate it and reward him, you will be in a very good place to help him develop the skills he needs to truly show you love. He wants to, but remember that he has that haunting, unseen threat somewhere deep inside that he's only conscious of when it bursts to the surface. So that invisible, subconscious instinct makes it very intimidating. It's a distant place for him—a creeping shadow in the far recesses of his mind and heart. You'll have to be satisfied with little morsels for now and keep praying and working for the banquet ahead.

I recently spoke with the wife of a disconnected man who is trying very hard to connect. She shared a couple of stories about how hard he is trying and how she has encouraged him. Last year they were going to a large family event and he asked her how he could use the event to work on connecting. He had never really tried to connect at family events before, choosing rather to sit apart and watch from a distance. She suggested that he try to meet as many of the family members as possible and have conversations with them. He did and he really enjoyed it!

After the event, as they were driving back home, he asked her how he did. She told him he was great! He did a really good job at introducing himself to family members who didn't know him well. And then she artfully added, "I would suggest only one area for improvement." He was visibly worried. She said simply, "Next time you have a chance to meet and connect with new people, I would love to be by your side." Boom! He got it right away. He had spent the whole day meeting new people and, as it were, looking over his shoulder at her to see if she approved, rather than meeting them *with* her so they could share the moments. I suspect you are like this wise woman and want him to be connected but also want to be part of that connection!

SEX

Your spouse loves sex but it also scares him to death, though he probably isn't conscious of this truth. Sex is so intimate that he has to stay a heartbeat or two away from it. I used to get stress headaches after times of intimacy with my wife. I always wondered why, but now I know that it was because my delicate psyche couldn't handle the closeness. I wanted to be close to her. I enjoyed intimacy with her. But my subconscious was working overtime to keep my guard up so that I wouldn't become vulnerable.

Your man's fumbling attempts to open up to you in every way, to experience emotion as deeply as he can without letting his guard down, will often leave you unsatisfied at best and feeling dirty at worst.

Does it help you to read about what's going on in his mind and on the surface of his heart? I realize that if you've been hurt for a while, it can block your ability to identify with him and understand. I'm praying that God will lift the curtain a little, easing your pain enough to let you see his struggles. If you can get a glimpse of his fragility, then perhaps you can sense his love.

If you can read and take in what I've tried to explain about his love, if you can receive it for what it is meant to be—true love— and if you can rest in the promises of God to use you in your husband's life, then I think you are ready to move on to greater challenges.

God's goal in your man's life is for him to be a relationally connected man. Remember, disconnection is disobedience.

You have the power to help your disconnected man consciously begin to heal and to find his key to true love. The next chapter will give you tools for the task at hand.

Chapter 9

My Man Won't Read This

Ladies, remember that you have the power to help your man learn how to show love to you. If he takes the advice of my last chapter, which is addressed to him, then he is about to walk into a foreign land filled with mental treachery, emotional demons, and practical distractions of every kind. You have the skills to help him through that land to the fullness of your open heart.

I'm going to start by asking you to do some house cleaning of your own. If you will tend to the things that are within your grasp, you will be better prepared to help him. I know that there are some of you who are too emotionally damaged to be of much help to him. If so, that's okay. He can make it with the help of the Lord and good men who will challenge him, but it may take longer if you are not able to pitch in from time to time.

You may have some anger or bitterness due to years of neglect. You won't be able to help him if that clings to you. Humble yourself and confess it. God understands, but He doesn't allow us to stay where we are. In fact, He tells us in Ephesians 4:31 (NIV), "Get rid of all bitterness, rage and anger, brawling and slander, along with every form of malice." He knows that anger is sometimes appropriate, but He also knows how easy bitterness takes root.

He wants you to trust Him with the anger. Give it to Him and let Him wash you clean. Part of the pain you feel is from carrying those feelings for too long. Self-pity, shame, worthlessness, and other emotions and thought patterns may have gained a foothold as well. Ask the sweet Spirit of God to reveal everything to you.

Pray: *Father, please show me any hindrance or barricade to the healing You have for me. I give these feelings to You. I release them. Help me to pray for my husband and put those things I can't yet forgive on a shelf for a while, while You work in me. Amen.*

This battle will require your complete attention.

The apostle Peter instructs women in your shoes to "be submissive to your own husbands so that even if any of them are disobedient to the Word, they may be won without a word by the behavior of their wives" (1 Peter 3:1, NASB). Ladies, the Bible says your husband can be won! He won't be won by some false idea of what submissiveness means. He will be won because you are honoring God by adorning yourself with the fruit of the Spirit—leading you to pursue your husband's healing. You have the power to win him if you adorn yourself with the attitude Peter describes.

Peter is not describing a wallflower here, but rather an incredibly strong woman who is willing to submit herself to God as her first lover and to her husband as her second. He is describing a woman who is willing to sacrifice her way for God's way. He is describing a creature of such incredible beauty and character that she can win a man's heart by her behavior. *That* is power.

Peter is not saying that you should be silent. He's promising that your *actions*, not your tongue, are the effective weapons in this warfare. The advice I'm going to give you includes using your voice but doing it in the spirit of Peter's instruction—with a gentle and submissive heart, wanting only the best for both you and your husband. God has given you a velvet hammer and He encourages you to use it.

As you submit everything you need to God, trusting Him to provide because he is faithful (Psalm 89:8), you can help this man. You've perhaps seen him as a bully or a brick wall or a betrayer up until now. I want you to see him as a little boy trying to be a man. If you react negatively to seeing him as a boy, you may need to revisit the first couple of steps. You must see him through gentler eyes before you can help him. Connection is a sign of maturity. An inability to connect means that something is immature and broken. Can you see him that way?

I first want to address those of you who are reading this alone. Your mate is not interested or involved yet. He doesn't think he has a problem and he's not interested in reading some "self-help nonsense." Your road is tough, but you can walk it and you will see God win in His time. Your approach will have to be delicate and crafty, but sure. You will have to be a master communicator in a language your man can understand. Remember that if any woman lacks wisdom, let her ask of God, who gives to all women liberally without teasing them for asking (James 1:5).

Your first responsibility is to pray as Hannah prayed in 1 Samuel 1. Pour out your blistered heart to God afresh. Let your whole soul spill out at His feet. Don't hold anything back. Tell Him all your hopes, dreams, and disappointments. Pray for the God of heaven to sweep down in mercy and bring all His energy to bear on your man's barricaded affections. Do not let go of God until He grants your petition.

Then ask yourself, "What do my man and I do best together?" It could be something as simple as taking a leisurely drive, gardening, or enjoying the same Netflix show. You can reach out regardless of the activity. Remind yourself that he does love you—he just has terrible difficulty showing you in ways that connect with your heart.

I've referred to a "good man" several times, and you may be wondering what I mean by that. I mean that your disconnected man is not evil. He doesn't have bad motives or ill desires for you or anyone else. He's a Christian (or not) who is trying to do the right thing. He is generally honest and caring. He's not a rebel. He's not revolting against God or good. At worst, he's simply a guy who gets up and goes about his business every day without a thought about what it all means. He doesn't know that he's disconnected, but he does try to be his best self. That's the kind of man who will benefit from your gentle persuasions.

Next time you are enjoying what you do best together and you feel as close to him as you ever do, tell him. Sincerely. Tell him how it fills you up emotionally to feel close to him. Tell him exactly what he did to help you feel close—he doesn't know, so he needs to be told. Maybe it was a look, or his tone of voice, or a particularly insightful mention of something you were feeling. Whatever it is, point it out. Please don't dismiss me here in favor of the old voices that keep telling you that he *should know*— I'm telling you that he doesn't know. He has to be instructed in the ways of your heart, and you are the only one with enough at stake to teach him.

Watch his response. Most men will puff a bit with pride. We really want to meet your needs and when we get something right, we are thrilled we succeeded. The response might not show up on any scale you can measure, but it will feel to him like a ton of gold has tipped his.

Conversely, tell him when you feel distant. This takes particular skill and wisdom. Don't do this in an offhanded or manipulative way. It could set all your efforts back a great deal. You can squash his ego if you are not careful. Men are often unpredictable when they feel shamed, so be genuine without being demanding. Beg God for help on this one. I could give you some hints, but your man is your man and I could be way off the mark. God will give you the perfect approach for the sensitivities of your mate if you are patient and trust Him. Don't neglect this out of fear, though. Your disconnected man needs to know the difference between when you feel connected and when you feel distant. Over time he will learn to recognize the difference and will realize he likes being connected much better than he likes being on the outside looking in.

A warning: Don't expect too much. You may have to repeat

this over and over before you get a real connection going. His emotional circuits are dormant from lack of use. A lot of energy may have to pass through before any spark lights. Keep returning to your power source in prayer for renewal. God will give you the strength to continue. If you allow your expectations to get too high, you run the risk of discouragement (Philippians 4:6).

For the women who are reading this with their man—good job to both of you. The instructions are much the same. The amazing thing is that even though the man knows what you are doing, it will have the same effect. (We're goofy that way.) We thrive on the praise and respect of our wives and we really do want to connect, though it scares us. Ladies, remember that your mate has engaged in a battle that is (in some ways) destroying him. Everything but his God and you are against him winning. He will want to quit and go back to the comfort of his shielded heart. He doesn't want to feel the pain of vulnerability. He doesn't like feeling out of control emotionally. He wants to tamp down the unfamiliar feelings of connectedness. It feels like it's going to gush out in ways he can't do anything about and that scares him.

Give him some space when he needs it. Keep cheering. Keep telling him how great he's making you feel. Keep praying for him. Keep respecting him for trying. Keep open to him. Keep disappointment at bay. Hold on tight despite failures. Keep telling him how much you admire him. Keep praying. Keep praying. Keep praying.

It may not seem like much to tell him when you feel connected or that you respect him, but I can assure you that your words offered in the right spirit will crack and crumble the buttresses holding up the walls around his emotions. Good men cannot withstand the power of right-spirited wives using their words to bring glory to God and honor to their husbands.

Ladies, as you start the work on your side of things, I want to encourage you to let your disconnected man read the next chapter first. If you read it, keep it to yourselves or between yourselves and the Lord in prayer. It's meant for the disconnected man. Your temptation, if you read it, will be to hold the truths written in it over his head like some sort of unreachable goal, or to secretly despise him for not achieving his calling. It's really not your place to do either. If the Holy Spirit is not ready to work this work in your man's heart, then your man is probably not ready yet. That doesn't mean he won't be someday. God is perfect and He fathers each of us perfectly. If your mate isn't ready, then God is content to wait. Are you?

If you're a man reading this, especially a disconnected man, then read on. If you only read one chapter of this book, the next one is it. The truth revealed in it is in many ways the glue that holds everyone together. One of our issues as disconnected men is that our glue never got a chance to set. We are in very real ways detached from everything God created us to be fastened to.

Chapter 10

If Men Read Only One Chapter...

If you are a disconnected man, you are walking in constant disobedience to nearly every command of Scripture. Obedience is about us reflecting God's desire to be intimately connected. It's not a duty or performance indicator—it's heartfelt relationship maintenance.

This statement is the cornerstone truth of your life. I make it without reservation because I think that God makes it without reservation in many ways throughout the Bible. You may be thinking, *How can Jim make such a bold statement about my condition before God? How does being disconnected keep me from being obedient? I don't remember any commands about "connection" in the Bible. What does connection have to do with the other commands of God?*

As humans created in God's image, we have a soul, a spirit,

a thinking mind, and an emotional heart. You are part of that human reality but are only precariously clinging to it. The reality is that humanity is held together by Relationship. Further, these relationships are intimate, personal, emotional, and communicative. Your inability to engage in intimate relationship has you perched at the craggy edge of true humanity.

Notice that I didn't say you couldn't do relationship at all. I'm sure you have lots of relationships: friends, family, acquaintances, and associates, but they are most likely only an inch deep. You could walk away from them without feeling the loss. That's not really relationship. True relationship has the ability to hurt you. If you lose a friend or loved one, you feel like you've lost a part of yourself. True relationships can elate you and take you to places of profound joy. Have you ever experienced that? Your disconnectedness prohibits it, but by God's grace you can begin to feel true loss or profound joy.

"But I love God," you might argue, "and I try to obey Him." I know. I said the same thing. God didn't necessarily call me a liar for saying it, but He did reveal to me that I was living in a fog of self-justification that kept me from seeing the clear crystal center of the universe, the glue that holds everyone together—Relationship. My love and obedience to God was offered up with such corruption and blemish that it was no better than giving Him pickings off the trash heap. My offering of "doing my duty" was to obey the letter of the law but totally miss the spirit. Much like the Pharisees (Matthew 23:23), I was blind to that fact, but blindness doesn't really excuse sin, does it? Once I was given eyes to see, I had no recourse but to repent and beg God to forgive me. Of course He did, gladly.

Once I saw that I really couldn't be right with God or man without the ability to have intimate relationships, I started on a road to true freedom and usefulness. This may all sound like mystical mumbo jumbo to you at the moment, but read on and I'll show you through Scripture what I mean. The ability to have a close relationship with God is the key to obeying Him and being covered by His righteousness. Nothing else substitutes. Here's why.

Let's start with the foundation of God's communication to His people in Israel through Moses. God spoke to Moses face-to-face, as a man speaks with a friend. In one of those face-to-face meetings, He gave Moses the Ten Commandments. I don't know what you've thought about those commandments in your life, but I want to point out that they are all about relationship. Take a look:

1. ***You shall have no other gods but Me.*** This is God commanding exclusive relationship. No distraction, no disloyalty, no disconnection. But I see this also as an invitation. God is saying that He wants a true connection with us and it breaks His heart if we wander away. He feels the loss. A cursory reading of the Old Testament will show you God's reactions to Israel's rebellion. Remember the golden calves Israel made in the wilderness? God was truly angry! Read Exodus 32:31 through Chapter 33 to see just how severe God is with sin but how gently and intimately He speaks with Moses.

2. ***You shall not make idols.*** Idols are false representations of reality. Idols don't talk, feel, communicate, or connect.

God does. He is real and relational. He spoke to Moses, Abraham, David, Samuel, Solomon, Adam, and a host of others. He maintained relationships. Idols can't do that. They are a poor, sad substitute for God, and so He forbids them.

3. *You shall not take the name of the Lord your God in vain.* Names are identifiers of persons. God is saying that He is high and holy and His name is above all other names. To treat His name flippantly is to dishonor and disrespect His person. What does that do to relationship? Have you ever had anyone show contempt toward you and then expect you to have a close relationship with them? People who are willing to disrespect God are essentially saying they don't need Him—they don't want a relationship with Him. Romans 1:21 tells us that even though mankind *knew* God, they did not glorify Him. They actually know God but show contempt for Him and His name. If relationship wasn't important to God, then why would He care what you did with His name?

4. *Remember the Sabbath day, to keep it holy.* This is the day set aside unto the Lord so that His people would be able to rest and meet with Him. This was a special day to connect with God and adore Him. *Connection* and *adoration* are relational words. They speak of intimacy and invitation. "Draw near unto Me and I will draw near to you" (James 4:8), He invites.

5. *Honor your father and mother.* This is the primary relationship of life, and God tells us to honor it. God doesn't qualify this based on what kind of parents we have. In other words,

He is instructing us to give our parental relationship worth and develop it.

6. **You shall not murder.** This is the ultimate sin against a human relationship. It is the absolute destruction of connection.

7. **You shall not commit adultery.** This is the second in line after murder as the destruction of a human relationship. And in fact, to commit adultery is to damage a relationship as completely as if you killed it.

8. **You shall not steal.** To steal from someone not only dishonors them or dismisses them, but it also breaks trust at such a primal level that connection again is all but impossible without true repentance and forgiveness.

9. **You shall not bear false witness against your neighbor.** Again, lying is like stealing. It breaks trust so severely that only through repentance and forgiveness can there be restoration.

10. **You shall not covet.** To covet is to want what someone else has—loving the thing more than the person. To put more value on an object than a relationship is truly disconnected. Acts 8:18 and following tells the story of a guy named Simon who wanted to buy the power of the Holy Spirit. He wanted the gift and not the person. Check it out; it didn't go well for him.

What about the Golden Rule: "Do unto others as you would have them do unto you"? Or check out Psalm 102 and the language of relationship used there. "Hear my prayer, O LORD! Let my cry for help come to You. Do not hide your face from me. Incline Your ear to me. Answer me quickly. My heart has been smitten. I have become like a lonely bird. Because of Your indignation and Your wrath. You will arise and have compassion." Read psalm after psalm and you will find relational communication. Deep wounding and abounding joy are both there for us to see what real relationship with God looks like.

Cut the Bible anywhere and it bleeds relationship.

God's laws are the boundaries around our relationship with Him. Move outside the boundaries and we move outside the relationship. Stay within the boundaries and we stay close to the heart of God. Every verse in the Bible is tied to relationship in some way. Some are about our relationship with our Heavenly Father, or His Son, or His Spirit, and the rest are about our relationships with others.

We don't sin against some arbitrary law written in emotionless stone interpreted by an unseeing, unfeeling, unheeding robot. We sin against God and against His love and provision for us. We sin against His Son and His Spirit. We sin against a person and against a relationship. To see and read the Bible in any other light renders it cold and legalistic—it becomes a chain to bind us to a heartless dictator who seeks obedience only to fulfill a lust for power. If that's our view of the Holy Scriptures and of God, then we are miserable creatures indeed.

But we don't have a relationship with a sightless, senseless, heartless God. We are drawn up into our God, who is "gracious, and full of compassion; slow to anger, and of great mercy" (Psalm 145:8). If you were to do a study and list all the character attributes of God, you would find that they are all relational. They all have something to do with the way He relates first to the Trinity, then to you and me and the rest of His creation.

Our God *is* relationship. We read it in the Bible as "God is love." What is love without a relationship in which to express it? Nothing. What is your life without relationships? Nothing. That's why I repeat, "If you are a disconnected man, you are walking in constant disobedience to nearly every command of Scripture."

- How can you make disciples in obedience to Christ's command (Matthew 28:19) if you don't enter into relationships? *You can't.*
- How can you love your wife as Christ loved the church (Ephesians 5:25) if you don't engage in deep intimacy with her? *You can't.*
- How can you love God with all your heart, soul, mind, and strength (Luke 10:27) if you are afraid of close connection? *You can't.*
- How can you diligently teach your sons when sitting and walking and lying down and rising up (Deuteronomy 6:4–10) if you have no relationship with them? *You can't.*
- How can you love your brothers and walk in the light (1 John 2:11) without relationship? *You can't.*

There is not one command of Scripture you can keep unless you are woven tightly into the fabric of God's life as well as the lives of those He's placed close to you. Intimate, personal Relationship is essentially, elementally indispensable. It is the irreducible minimum of the sentient universe. If you are disconnected, you are barely clinging to the ragged edge of reality.

The truth is inescapable, but the question remains: What are you going to do about it? I know you are a doer. You can accomplish amazing things. I should probably rephrase the question and ask, "How are you going to *feel* this?" I could give you a list of objectives to accomplish, steps to take, or a plan to become relational, and I'm sure you would excel at ticking off all the boxes. But I fear you would remain nonrelational and disconnected.

It might help if I relate how I experienced this truth. When my wife left me, I had already started becoming relational and so was meeting regularly with several of my closest male friends. But when my wife told me that she wanted a divorce, I intentionally avoided those same friends because I knew I needed to feel the pain, and meeting with them would only have lessened it. They had a way of comforting me that would have reduced the bitterness I needed to feel. So I isolated myself to feel.

In those months, I was ground to powder in the crucible of grace. I wish I could say days, but it took me many months to work through. I opened myself up to every molten memory that wanted to sear away my forgetfulness. I made myself remember the pain I had caused. I thrust every arrow of my wife's suffering words into my own heart again and again. I revisited every detail of my own pain that I could dredge out of my blighted past. I dwelt in sorrow. I meditated on sadness. I felt pain more deeply than I had ever felt it before. I let it in. I let it burn me and scar me. I let it blast and purify me. I thrust myself on God. I didn't ask Him to take away the grief or the injury. I allowed the intensity to burrow in and the suffering to linger. I knew that if I didn't walk this valley of death, I wouldn't die. But I had to die in order to live again. And I wanted to live. I wanted to relate, to feel, to hurt, to be happy, to connect. So I suffered and endured. The wrath of my disconnected past flowed over me. But I began to feel freedom with every wave that broke and rolled over me. I began to feel clean and loved and beckoned to. I began to feel that God was picking up the threads of my misery and weaving them into the borders of His garment. I felt like I could look into His eyes and let Him love me. I wasn't afraid of the intimacy anymore. I was being healed. I am still being healed.

Perhaps you'll have to visit the same place I did—the dreadful inner chambers of your broken and wounded heart. I can tell you that if you decide to go there, you will not go alone. God is already there, calling for you to come. He has been there all along and He already exists on the other side of your pain. He has passed through and He waits for you to follow. So the question remains, "How are you going to *feel* this?" You need to feel it, brother. You don't need to *do* anything about it—you need to sense it and let it touch the raw nerves of your hidden heart. Otherwise you will continue to live in a knowing disobedience. You will be a rebel to righteousness. You will clench a fist of mutiny in the face of the captain of your soul.

Maybe you won't need to have an experience like mine. Perhaps you can simply decide to obey and then somehow become relational. I hope you can. I truly hope that you can discover how to relate without going through the pain of metamorphosis. If God will spare you that, then He deserves your highest praise. Whatever the pathway for you, I hope you enter it soon. There are loved ones waiting for you. Don't take the road of denial. Be a valiant warrior and face the battle.

I think you are a good man, with no desire to turn from God. I think you may also be so frightened by the ghouls you'll find behind the walls of your pain that you don't want to go there. I implore you to go anyway. It's the only way. Be brave and start. God will carry you after the first step.

Once you enter, suffer, and exit these corridors of rebirth, you will have to learn to walk again. The next chapter will give you some helpful hints for crawling toward connectedness. This is also when you may find some help from your loving wife.

Chapter 11

Crawling Toward Connection

I don't want you to think of yourself as a baby here. That's not the kind of crawling I think is needed. It's more the crawl of a wounded warrior dragging himself off the battlefield to a safe place. If you enlisted in the war I described in the last chapter and you've fought battles that are helping you to feel something, then you can probably picture the kind of crawling I'm referring to. If you are dying to yourself (as this battle demands), then your wounds are deep, you've lost a lot already, and you are feeling weak and exhausted. Walking is not an option.

When you've fought and won a relentless battle against malicious and powerful foes, it is an honor to pull your broken self off a battlefield in victory. Crawling is not something to be ashamed of. You will have to make slow and deliberate moves to develop skills you haven't exercised in the past. You may have to go at a speed that is uncomfortably sluggish for a doer and results-oriented guy like yourself. You are also healing from some nasty wounds that are likely to make your trip slower. Get comfortable with the pace; it's important that you don't hurry this process.

I'm a systematic thinker, so I tend to lay things out in a definite order. Below is the path I've followed up to now to become more relational. It may not be the best path for you, but you should get enough ideas of what the road looks like to make a good start. I think that if you read, meditate, and pray about your approach, the Lord will be faithful to help you start and then give you each step at the appropriate time. By the way, none of the suggestions below will help much unless you are meeting daily with your Savior. If you are not burying yourself in God's Word and prayer, then the rest will be of only marginal help. Here's how my journey looked. Notice that every step involves people. (You can't become relational without them!)

Meet regularly, one-on-one, with godly men. This was a natural step for me since it was one of my male friends who pointed out my relational disconnectedness. He was the first one I met with regularly. I soon added a couple more. I think it's crucial to start with men. They understand most of what you are experiencing and can identify with you in ways that most women cannot. It's safer, and progress happens faster. Things were pretty raw at the start, because I was dealing with the fact that my wife had walked away and left me with all four of our children at home (a responsibility I had never had to bear on my own before). These men didn't look down their noses at me, even though they each had healthy marriages. That was important.

What you talk about is of secondary importance to how you feel about the topic or relate to it. With my friends and me, it was sometimes about being separated and then divorced. How my kids were feeling and handling it (I had to actually know how they were feeling, which was another part of this process, as you will see). How different people we knew were doing, and how I felt about it. How work was going or politics or my faith or sports. No matter what the topic, we were honest, which led to a lot of observations about my progress. Transparency is the key.

Determine to be completely transparent with these men regardless of what you are thinking or struggling with. My friends know everything about me now. I didn't hide anything then and I still don't. They know when I'm sad, frustrated, tempted, victorious, tired, poor, unfulfilled, and so on. The fact that they are godly men was essential, because they listened without judging me and I could share my struggles without fear of condemnation. I knew I could always walk away from our meetings without shame or feelings of inadequacy. I also knew they would remember our conversations and hold me accountable to them! They reciprocated by letting me into their world as well.

Having these men insist on real relationship is necessary. My friends wouldn't let a week go by without hearing from me or having coffee with me. They dug in and asked hard questions and told me when they felt I was avoiding an issue. They were crawling along with me. These are true brothers. I believe they will stand by me in any battle because we are now connected. Now I know I would suffer if I were to lose one of them.

On one occasion, I got a piece of very difficult news, so I

stopped into the office of one of these men. He was extremely busy, so I merely exchanged pleasantries with him and told him to have a good day. Later that day he found out about my news from another source. I immediately received an urgent text from him, demanding that we meet for coffee the next morning. When we met, he was angry. He was angry with me for stopping by to see him with something heavy on my heart, but then letting his busyness keep me from telling him. He made it crystal clear to me that no matter what was happening, he was there for me. But I had to do my part.

The second safe place for me while I was crawling was with my children. I have the privilege of being a father to four of the most genuinely happy and honest kids a man could have. It helped tremendously that they were young adults, so I could explain to them what I was learning and they could understand. I shared with them what I was discovering about myself and apologized to them for the damage it had caused them over the years. They forgave me and helped me grow.

Even though they were suffering from the loss of their mother, they were willing to join me on my journey. My daughters were especially helpful in engaging with me and pointing out when they felt I was being relational and when I wasn't. The insights they gave me were truly amazing. I remember becoming angry with one of my sons to the point where it brought him to tears (I think he was twenty at the time), and then realizing that my anger was due to my own failure to communicate. My daughter gently but firmly said to me, "You can't do that anymore, Dad." She was right and I needed to hear it. I had to relate and not control.

My boys were not far behind in pointing out when I fell into my old nonrelational habits. My youngest son was especially insightful and took the time to explain after something I said or reacted to. He actually explained how it made him and perhaps others feel. There was one time we both pointed out a few things we were feeling about his mom. He confronted me and I confronted him and then he sat on my lap and we cried together. If you have older children, then bring them into your world and allow them to speak to your heart. You will benefit.

If you have younger children, then simply spend time with them. Listen to them and try to feel what they are feeling, especially if they are little girls. They will tell you what is still in your wife's heart. Listen to their little princess dreams—they are the same ones your wife has always hoped you would listen to. Regardless of how disconnected and unavailable you've been in the past, you are still their hero and the man of their imagination. For your small boys, you are the mountain they are moving toward. You are the champion they hope to become. You are the image of what they see as manhood. The image is obviously tarnished if you've been disconnected, but you now have the ability to change all of that. In you, they see God, or the reflection of who God is supposed to be. As you become relational in the way God is, they will become rich and relational as well, and hopefully avoid many of the troubles you've experienced.

Another safe place for me to learn was with a Christian counselor, a godly older man who had been through much of what I was experiencing, even suffering a failed marriage in the same way and for many of the same reasons I did. Men like him are rare. If you can find one, run, don't walk, to learn from him. Having someone trained in biblical counseling is a marvelous blessing and a great help.

I don't know enough about professional, classically trained counseling to say whether it would be of help. The stigma of professional counseling may be a challenge for you as well, but by all means, if God tells you to do it, you should. Get help anywhere you can.

Your extended family may or may not be of help. I think I might have gotten some help from one or two of my family members, but they were too far away and the shock of what was happening with my marriage would probably have been too distracting. Your family dynamics may make family members the best helpers in this situation, or they could be the worst enemies—barricades to healing and moving forward. Be very careful here. Some families will tell you it's all in your head and you don't need to do anything. Some will react with offense and take it that you are personally accusing them of causing or playing a part in your disconnectedness. Some will pity you and attack your wife or friends or church.

If your extended family is supportive and for the most part healthy, then they may play an important role in your progress. Think of mature, preferably godly, family members who have wisdom and compassion. Go to them and let them know what you are working through. Ask them to observe you and let you know when you are being relational, humble, engaging, or something positive and different from who you've been before. Having other eyes on your situation will help you learn what it feels like to connect.

I am sorry to say that I couldn't get any help from my wife.

She was already too badly damaged to enter into this world with me. I will say this, though. *If your wife is willing to crawl with you, then let her.* There will be much temptation for her along the way. She may be tempted to become impatient, or to react negatively to discovering more than she wants to know, or any number of other things. It may also be very difficult for you to let her in at this point. If in the presence of God you feel it is beneficial, then invite her to travel with you. If you feel a warning in your spirit, then wait.

This may be a good place to remind you of all the pain that you caused her and the boomerang effect it has had on you. Your former disconnection caused her to shut down, which may now be causing you great pain. Regret waits for you when you lay your head on the pillow at night, it's the first thing to greet you when you wake up in the morning, and it creeps along behind you, marking every step of your day. The nagging question that kept scratching on the chalkboard of my mind in the early days of discovery was, "What if it's too late?"

I've now come to believe that "too late" is an excuse for "not willing." The challenge is for both parties to remain willing. The question often remains, "What if she isn't willing?" That is for your wife to decide. Your decision, as a man of God who is determined to obey, is to get up every morning and be different from any man you've ever been before. It's not your mission to win her back. It's your mission to do what's right. If her heart changes, then your life will indeed be blessed—you will have the relationship she always craved and you've always needed. If it doesn't, you will have an intimacy with your Father that you had no idea was possible. Either way, you will come through the fire a refined, relational, obedient man and one day find yourself saying it was worth the suffering.

There is one thing I must sternly warn you about: DO NOT engage in relationship with other women. You are emotionally vulnerable, and sharing intimate details about relationship struggles can leave you open to connections that God forbids. It also tempts the woman you are sharing with to use her natural nurturing instincts to help you. This can lead to improprieties beyond the boundaries of your present relationship. You will invite nothing but trouble into your life if you take this road.

If you feel that another woman's insight would be extremely helpful about some aspect of your situation, then ask her in a group setting or when her husband is present. Or ask her husband to ask her. This is safe and will not lead to relationship ties you will regret for the rest of your life. Don't cross this line.

Once you have started connecting with others, you will need to get feedback. Since you really aren't good at *feeling* connected, you may not know if you are. You will need others to tell you when they feel connected. They may have to describe it to you. You need to make it clear to them that they will literally have to point out to you when you've done something relational. In order for them to help you, they will have to know what you are asking them to do. Here is a short list of suggestions you could make to help them notice the right things:

1. Ask them to tell you when they notice you exercising a generally different approach to people. Ask them to tell you if they felt it was sincere. Have them share with you how they thought the other person responded.

2. Ask them to describe in detail when they feel connected with you. Have them give you a full account of what made them feel that way.

3. Ask them to tell you if they sense more humility in you. Humble people connect better.

4. Have them watch for red flags. It could be a rising frustration they sense in you. It could be depression. It could be that they see you slipping back into old patterns. Have them tell you everything, even if it's just a misty impression with no tangible evidence.

5. Tell them to ask you hard questions, such as, "Does that interaction make you feel uncomfortable? Did you know you were rude back there? Did you cry at that part of the movie? You just treated your daughter badly; did you know it? Did you see how your son lit up when you said that you were proud of him?"

You might think of other things pertinent to your life that will help here. Add them to the list. Keep adding and keep listening until you sense more relationship. Eventually you will instinctively know when you are connecting. It's a great feeling of accomplishment. Once we connect and get through the fear of connecting, then we begin to discover beautiful vistas of living we never could have imagined when we were disconnected.

The most surprising thing for me has been how appreciated I feel by those around me. This may be the hardest thing I've had to get used to. I didn't know how much people needed me because I didn't truly feel a need for them. Once the need was awakened in me, I started seeing how precious I was to them. I don't think I ever would have felt such profound feelings of being loved and needed if I hadn't started deliberately connecting with those around me. It has been extremely humbling and incredibly joyful.

And the greatest reward? The closeness I feel with my Heavenly Father. I have a hard time reading any part of the Bible now without weeping. It doesn't take much to start the waterworks. My heart is extremely sensitive to the emotions of God. I feel the betrayal of His people. I hurt for Him. I grieve for the damage done by and to biblical characters. I sense His love for me and His disappointment. I *feel* close to Him. You will too.

Don't fool yourself, though. This is not an overnight trip, and it's not a smooth road. Sometimes it will feel like driving a Humvee through a minefield. You will need immense patience with yourself and with others. Others will have to be patient with you as well.

Chapter 12

Patience Lasts a Long Time

A man cannot turn a lifetime of relational numbness into passionate interaction overnight.

I know that many of you ladies have already waited nearly a lifetime for something to come along and breathe life into your disconnected man so he could breathe life into you. You have agonized, wept, poured your heart out to God, stomped your feet, and bit your tongue. Now that there's some hope of change, it will be very difficult to let the change happen in its time. But you must. Patience must become your primary virtue if you want to maintain your relationship with your disconnected man while he's learning to connect.

The Bible is packed with admonitions and encouragements to wait: "Wait on the LORD: be of good courage, and he shall strengthen thine heart: wait, I say, on the LORD" (Psalm 27:14).

See also Isaiah 40:31; James 5:7–8; John 5:6; Lamentations 3:25; 2 Peter 3:9; Psalm 37:34; and Psalm 130:5–6.

The Bible is also full of stories of those who didn't wait: Eve didn't wait for Adam before taking the fruit. Abraham didn't wait on God to give him a son. Lot's daughters didn't wait for God to provide them mates. Aaron and the children of Israel didn't wait on Moses to come down from the mountain. Saul didn't wait on Samuel before he sacrificed to God.

We could give more examples but I think you get the point. Nothing good happens when we fail to wait on God. Remember, though, that waiting is not passive hand-wringing until something miraculous happens. Waiting is an active grace that requires you to stay busy about the things God has called you to do. Perhaps you should be asking God, "How can I wait fruitfully?" If you constantly give your complaints and impatience to God and ask Him to keep your hands, mind, and heart busy, He will answer that prayer. I can offer some suggestions to keep you busy while you persevere. Ask God if any of these apply and then pursue them with all the energy you have:

- *Spend valuable time with intimate family and friends.* Don't skimp on this. Get away as often as you can to invest in your friends and to allow them to invest in you. Friendships and family can be incredibly strong ballasts to keep you upright while you wait. Don't neglect them. Share your burdens with them without gossiping. If your disconnected man is on a road toward relationship, then ask your friends to pray with you for his success. Let God love you through them.

- **Spend time absorbing your children.** By *absorbing*, I mean stop being a mom for a while and just watch the beautiful little creations God has placed in your hands. Soak in their innocence. Watch them laugh and play. Take every little giggle and twirl into your heart. Listen for every car and heavy machine noise your sons make and pray for their manhood. Let the rays of their childhood warm you. Drift off with them to imaginary lands. Get lost in the simple delights of childhood.
- **If your children are older, devote yourself to raising them.** Spend time filling up the cups of their souls with yourself. You are valuable. They need your soul to be poured into theirs. They need your spirit and wisdom. Walk with them, ski with them, bowl with them, swim with them, cook with them—whatever it takes to be around them, do it. You will never regret time spent filling them up.
- **See a counselor.** There are some things too heavy to bear alone and too confidential to tell your friends. Find a godly counselor who will listen and ask good questions. Let them draw out all your hidden fears so you can submit them to God. Let them watch you cry. Let them point you to the Lord.
- **Find a God-ordained hobby or ministry.** Be careful that it doesn't overwhelm you or steal time that should be spent elsewhere. Give God all your talents and gifts to use as He sees fit. Teach others when you can. Serve everyone you can. God loves a cheerful giver.
- **Disciple someone.** This might sound difficult. How can you invest in someone else when your relational cup isn't being

filled up? You can. The Lord reminds us that He is our provider. He gives us everything we need. He is the Lover of our soul. His supply is enough. He fills your cup to overflowing. Take some of the overflow and give other thirsty souls a drink. You will find that as you give of yourself the waiting becomes easier.

- *Exercise.* Do as little as take a walk or as much as run a marathon. Get your blood pumping and keep yourself healthy. A healthy body helps your mind cope. It helps you endure emotional stress. It occupies your time. It gets you into the sunshine. It builds your energy and helps you fight every kind of battle.
- *Encourage your husband.* I have no way of knowing how saying this affects you. It may incite an immediate breakdown. It might make you angry. It could energize you. It could cause you to slide into depression. It could make you laugh. It could break you into a million pieces. It might even warm your heart to a glow. I don't know. I just know that you need to do as much of it as you possibly can.

You see, dear sister, your husband is suffering. I understand that you have suffered, too, maybe for years. You suffer because you know what should be. You can feel it. He suffers because he's missing everything that's real. He can't feel anything. I'm asking you again to see him through merciful and pitying eyes. If he's trying to become relational, then he's feeling pains he has no idea what to do with. He's experiencing hurt that has no place to go in his soul. It sticks and lingers in places that grate against his raw nerves. He is dying, and it will help him to have you at his bedside while his old self passes. He will need you to help revive him when his relational heart starts to show signs of life.

The greatest trial of patience is showing it to those who have caused your pain. Think of Jesus. He endured the cross, despising the shame, because there was joy set before Him (Hebrews 12:2). The passage goes on to say, "Consider Him who has endured such hostility by sinners against Himself, so that you will not grow weary and lose heart" (Hebrews 12:3). Is that verse about you? Does it seem that you could substitute your name for Christ's and your husband's name for *sinners?* There may be times when you feel so sinned against that no other thought can break through. You can't see or anticipate joy and you can't break the stranglehold of past pain. This passage is the balm for that kind of pain.

Starting at verse 1, this passage invites you to do three things: (1) Lay aside every encumbrance and sin that so easily entangles you, (2) run with endurance the race that is set before you, and (3) fix your eyes on Jesus. There is a raging temptation to see your circumstances through sinful eyes and then make sinful decisions as a result. Your Father asks you to lay those things aside. Loosen your grasp on the anger and bitterness of your loss. The tighter you grip it, the more it eats into your hand. You may have to do this many times. Sinful patterns have a tendency to cling to us. Hurt caused by perceived wrong can stick to your heart like glue. You'll likely have to repeatedly go to Jesus with it for cleansing. In essence, you have to lay down your right to hold the injury against your man or against God.

After laying down your rights to revenge for the injuries you've suffered, you'll have to run. Running with the weight of sin hanging from you is not very practical. Once those things that easily entangle and trip you are discarded, though, you can run with endurance, free of burdens. There is a race set before you. The end goal is that you become holy. The path is one of long-suffering and determined effort. The goal is Christ.

Only Jesus can give you the strength to get through. That's why the last thing that God requires of you is to rivet your gaze upon the wounded and suffering Christ. Jesus, who was shamed without cause. Jesus, who endured the hostility of those He fashioned with His own hands. Jesus, who felt the betrayal of those He dearly loved. Jesus, who despised the humiliation forced upon Him at the hands of brutal rebels. Jesus, who unjustly languished under cruel abuse. Jesus, lover of my soul while I was a sinner and when I despised everything good and beautiful. It is that Jesus we look to in our hour of greatest temptation. When we want satisfaction for our pain. When we want revenge. When we can't endure. When we faint and fall on the course. It is that Jesus who captures our gaze and gives us life to continue. Only Jesus can help you through your ordeal, sister. Fix your eyes on Jesus. He will bear you all the way through.

Don't let my mention of your man's battle detract from the fact that you are cared for by your Heavenly Father. He sees and He weeps. He draws you up to His chest and cradles you in everlasting love. He wipes the tears from your eyes and holds you in tender caress. Wait there in His embrace. Live out the days of your patience encircled by His arms. Staying there will never grow old and days will pass more sweetly. Wait there. Rest.

While you are doing your part and your man is doing his and God is superintending the entire effort, there will come a day when man and woman and their God will have the joy of running this race together.

Chapter 13

Arm in Arm

My dear brother and sister, I'm assuming that you are both treading this path together. For the sisters who are walking alone and gallantly attempting to help their man with little conscious cooperation from him, I hope you can take heart in this chapter. I hope you can see with the eyes of faith that this can be true. Please remember that I had to walk my path alone too. My wife was not with me. I understand your hopeful anguish. I understand your lonely toil. I understand the fight against hopelessness.

In spite of having traveled the path alone, what I'm about to write is real. I know it is, because there are thousands of couples who are satisfied together. They are connected, intertwined, inseparable, and joyfully happy. I marvel at them. I learn from them. I rejoice for them and with them.

I have learned much by observing and reading about such couples and how they maintain their love. I want to apply what I've learned to a couple emerging from a formerly disconnected existence into a thriving partnership. I don't want to present some ethereal idea of perfect bliss, borne aloft by fairy dust and angels. I want to share some daily disciplines that will help you maintain every new level of connectedness you reach. I want to give you practical and substantive everyday habits. The goal is to create and maintain connection and intimacy.

Ladies, though I can't see through your eyes, I'll do my best to give you something solid to hold on to. I think you have the intuitive gifts to see from your mate's perspective and respond well. God made you to nurture and love instinctively. When your man is doing the best he can to connect, I think that your heart naturally reciprocates.

Let's begin with the man who realized that he was disconnected and so took up the battle honorably and has been engaged in combat. Brother, make every attempt to connect that you can. Don't overthink it; don't contrive something just to satisfy the inner drive to accomplish. Pull things up from your emotional well and present them to your beloved. Hold them out to her and let her see. Tell her how you *feel* about things—anything. You can start with a news story, a tragedy or triumph. It could be some memory of an old movie that you've never shared. Maybe a childhood fear or difficulty. Maybe something about the kids, or your job, or a worry on your mind. It could be anything, but make a start. Start like this: "I'm afraid for our son. He isn't making good decisions. I'm worried that he's going to end up learning the hard way. It makes me regret not having a better relationship with him." You've just admitted you can be afraid, worried, and regretful—feelings we all experience that help others know what's going on inside.

Ladies, let's assume that an attempt to connect, no matter how lame, has been offered. At that moment, your disconnected man is as vulnerable as he has ever been. Vulnerability is terrifying to someone whose heart has been incarcerated in solitary confinement for any length of time. He is fragile. He is nervous. He wants to withdraw back to safety. He is so brittle in that moment that a wrong response could devastate him. He probably doesn't let on that he's feeling tentative or frail, but I assure you that he is.

Your part as his helpmate and lover is to respond with gentleness to his effort. Let yourself be enthralled and captivated by it. Be genuine, even if his effort is tiny and faltering. Open up to it. Appreciate it. Receive it. Tell him how much you appreciate it. Tell him how it fills up your heart to see him try. Respond to him and honor him for reaching out from his woundedness to minister to yours.

Don't just do this in the moment. Thank him later in the day. Tell him how it made you feel. Tell him that you felt connected in that moment. Linger over it. Remind him the next day that it was special. Don't let him forget how he touched you. Don't pander or fake it, but go as far as you honestly can.

Ask him how he felt and then listen intently. You'll pick up clues that will help you encourage him the next time he makes an attempt to connect.

For you ladies with husbands who are not trying to connect, you may be surprised that it works much the same way. It may be even more effective with the man who is not trying. If he does something to connect, he will not expect your response. If you respond as I just described, it will shock him positively. It will leave him wondering what in the world he did right. He will be confused, but he will be thrilled that he actually did something right and he'll want to do it again.

If a woman does this well, the man will come up to this level and stay there. His heart will open a bit. He will connect. If she reacts negatively, sarcastically, or as if in shock, she will set him back, and it might be a long while before another attempt is made. If she can't bring herself to respond rightly, she runs the risk of completely shutting him down for the foreseeable future.

Once a man steps up to a new level of intimacy, he will grow comfortable with it. That could be good or bad. If he's comfortable, he may see no need to push forward. But if he's comfortable at this level, he may be energized to try another step. It depends on many factors—all of them unique to the couple's circumstances. If he stagnates, then he may need some careful persuasion. God can give you wisdom on this one, ladies. If your man is openly trying to connect and you are working together, then you should be able to gently show him that he's stalled. When both of you work to uncover what is causing the delay, then you will probably find a way to take a new step forward.

After a few successful attempts at connection that are met with a positive response from you, there will come a time when your disconnected man will start to *feel*. He will start to sense connection. This is stunning progress. The only way to know when this happens is to stay in constant communication with each other about connection. You should have been discussing your relationship and your progress with each of his connection attempts. If you were, then the day will come when he will say that he *felt* something different. That day is monumental for both of you. If you are prone to mark days and keep records of special times, then you should write this one down. You should do something special to celebrate it.

Once your disconnected man feels it, owns the feeling, and learns to enjoy it, he will find freedom. This reality will break his chains and start to unlock all the doors in front of his heart. It's just the beginning, though. There may be a lot of hurt to work through as the doors unlock and swing open. But he now has the key. When his doors start swinging open, it may be difficult at that point for you to grow accustomed to your new man. You may need some time to adjust. It might be strange to be face-to-face with the man you've always desired and prayed for.

If your disconnected man doesn't fight these new feelings, he will soon find himself running to unlock every relational door he can find. Connection is a powerful drug. It's a painkiller. A lasting high. A muscle relaxer. A stress reliever. An aphrodisiac. Medicine for every antirelational ailment. Once he becomes addicted to relationship, he becomes addicted to life. Not only can he feel alive, but also he can now give life. He will be a fountain of living water for you to drink from. He will cry more. He will laugh more. He will smile authentically. He will see into your eyes and not just notice their color. He will start to wind the coils of his heart with yours.

All of this coming from your formerly disconnected man

may scare you to pieces. You won't know how to respond to it all and it will feel so bizarre that you'll want to run at times. Don't! Stay close and give yourself up to the connection. Once connected, you can't be unraveled. The best thing to do at this level is to satiate yourselves with one another. Talk, talk, talk. Spend lingering moments gazing into each other's eyes. Hold each other. Walk long walks. Drive long drives. Sit across the table from one another so you are face-to-face. Sit side by side on the love seat. Curl up on the couch. Cuddle in bed. Talk. (Did I say that already?) Lie hand in hand on the grass and gaze at the sky. Share your dreams. Laugh out loud. Cry often. Rub noses. Kiss and keep kissing. Pray together. Pray for lasting attachment. Pray for unbreakable bonds. Pray for absolute unity. Pray for love. Praise God who is love. Make the most of his new connection. Build on it daily and diligently.

This is where you fall in love again. Don't let it die. Write every memory on every calendar day and then task yourself to repeat the memories in the days to come. Keep throwing wood on the fire. Build a blaze that will last.

Light is the destroyer of darkness. Anything that lets light in should be obtained and added to this foundation of connection. The black walls of disconnection should be replaced with transparent crystal panes. You will both need to become see-through in order to maintain your connection and keep enemies from erecting their dark panels in the future.

Chapter 14

Become See-Through

Glass is amazing. It's solid and smooth and completely see-through. It protects us from wind and rain and yet allows us to see the beauty all around us. At the aquarium, it holds a vibrant and colorful environment together so we can admire all the life and activity within. Glass is a transparent housing for the most delicate of collectables, allowing us to appreciate them without any danger of spoiling or breaking them. Relationships should be like that.

Your relationships should be the glass that protects you from the storms of life and the blasts of the harsher elements while never obscuring the beauty of everything God has created. Glass should surround the delicate environment of your inner man without blocking the view into your heart. They should allow your loved ones to marvel at the finery of what makes you tick without the fear that they will somehow harm you. Relationships like that are worth pursuing.

What I've just described is probably rare even among relationally healthy couples. It's very difficult to maintain transparency and vulnerability without some sort of damage occurring along the way. That doesn't mean we shouldn't try. Now that our formerly disconnected man is able to relate, he can begin to become completely transparent. Much of what he has done to this point was like rubbing years of greasy dirt around to let some murky light through. After several cleanings, he is now beginning to see more light than dirt. Now we can move on to relational clarity.

Transparency in relationships is the quality of being able to share anything without fear of reprisal.

As transparency matures, it manifests itself in the lack of willingness for either party to do anything that would jeopardize the clarity. In the early stages, there can be a lot of dirt hidden in the shadows that when brought out will stain and hurt the relationship. As the days go by and the relationship becomes clean, there will be fewer and fewer opportunities for offense. All the surfaces will become clean, and each person can see the other's corners and crevices clearly. Each can savor the view into the other's heart. There is nothing to hinder the connection. Eventually communication becomes easy because one partner can clearly see what is already happening in the other's heart before it gets to his countenance. This sounds grand, doesn't it!

But for those who maintain shadows and dirt in the back rooms of their souls, it sounds scary. We don't want to be found out. We don't like light if we are hiding something. The key is to stop hiding the old things and start pursuing holiness so that in the future there will be nothing to hide. If you trip and fall, get dirty and stained, but the glass of your life is clear, then your partner will see it and offer to help clean you up. As lovers, our first reaction when seeing our loved one trip and fall should not be condemnation or ridicule. Our instinct should be to run and help, to clean and mend. Transparent people do this.

How do we maintain transparency? Fortunately God is not silent on the subject. He wants us to be clean and see-through. He certainly sees everything. Let's start with James 5:16: "Therefore, confess your sins to one another, and pray for one another so that you may be healed. The effective prayer of a righteous man can accomplish much."

This verse is deeper and richer than it appears on the surface. It is an invitation for each party to be transparent. The verse instructs us to confess to one another. That's a two-way street. Each person confesses their sins to the other. It starts with the one who has a particular sin to confess, though. The sinner has to become vulnerable. He can be vulnerable because he knows he's confessing to a "righteous man." A righteous man in this case is not a sinless man (or woman), but a sister or brother who is cleansed by the blood of Christ and is presently walking in obedience to Him. Their relationship with Christ is unbroken.

Once the sinner becomes vulnerable and clear about his sin and trusts that he has a faithful and forgiving ear to confess to, he can offer up his soul for cleansing. He can rest in the assurance that his brother or sister will forgive and aid in the cleansing process without condemnation. When we know that we can be made clean without fanfare or criticism, we are most likely to return time and time again for forgiveness. This freedom keeps the door open for transparency.

The righteous person has a unique responsibility in this transaction. He prays. Notice that God doesn't instruct him to do anything else. No lectures. No condemnation. No Bible lesson. No gossip. Just prayer. In fact, the instruction is that both get to pray for the other because both are sinners. Prayer in this case is the reaction that stops all of our fleshly reactions to sin. It is identifying with the sinner while kneeling at the foot of the cross where Christ forgave both sinners.

Isn't that a marvelous gift from God? He gave us a reaction that quiets all our human reactions: judgment, repulsion, distance, disgrace, or anger. God asks us simply to pray. I think this is partly so He can work grace, pity, mercy, forgiveness, and love more deeply into our hearts. Prayer causes us to pause and consider how we've benefited from the sacrifice of our Savior and allows us to see our own sin and stay on the same level as our brother or sister.

When two sinners are on the same ground praying for each other, God says that He can do great things.

Prayers of sinners who have been made righteous avail much! There is triumph and advantage in these prayers. Strongholds are breached and soul kingdoms are won by this kind of praying. Couples are held together in unbreakable bonds when they can pray for one another like this.

By the way, this is not an optional suggestion for formerly disconnected men and the women who love them. Neither of you get to withhold confession or prayer for one another. If you do, you risk sliding back into the dark abyss of disconnection.

Maintaining transparency requires that we speak the truth in love: "Therefore, laying aside falsehood, speak truth each one of you with his neighbor, for we are members of one another" (Ephesians 4:25). We belong to one another and to God, so we tell the truth. Lies are black walls around our hearts. Keep a lie and you become less transparent. Keep enough of them and you'll be back behind the walls of disconnection.

We need to be blunt here. Don't nuance, shade, spin, or complicate the truth. Humble yourself and speak it plainly. Be transparent.

Transparency is also maintained by revealing ourselves in total to our mates. Think of God. He gave us sixty-six books of transparent insight into His person. He opened Himself and His character up to our scrutiny. He lays it all out. We can see what makes Him happy, sad, angry, disappointed, honored, and connected. It's a risky thing to hold nothing back.

Become transparent, and your mate might recoil from something that frightens them. They might withhold a piece of their heart because they don't understand you. They might react in anger. They might cry. They might laugh at you. They might condemn. But they might want more. They might draw near. They might even intertwine with you so tightly that you can't distinguish yourself from them. Isn't that the ultimate risk, to lose yourself in your partner? Isn't that what Jesus prayed for in John 17:22? "The glory which You have given Me I have given to them, that they may be one, just as We are one." Can the Father be separated from the Son?

The practical application of all of this is a daily discipline. It is the discipline of taking the time to communicate. It is the discipline of sharing the things with your mate that bubble up from beneath the surface of your person. It is the practice of intimate conversation, of lingering communion. None of this happens by accident. We are busy people. We think of things and then something else pushes the thought out. We aren't in one another's vicinity often enough. We are separated by superhighways and office complexes, jet planes and conferences, school schedules and demanding employers.

But wait! Don't we live in the digital age of hypercommunication? We truly have more ways to reach out to one another than any age ever before. We can call, text, leave voice mails, e-mail, Facebook, Instagram, tweet, and Snapchat till our eyes are crossed and our brains are drained. We are all aware of the downside of these forms of communication, but there's an upside: We have instant communication. It may not be the same quality as face-to-face affection, but we can use it in so many ways. We can send reminders to our mate (or ourselves) that we have something to discuss this evening. We can simply say we are thinking about them. We can flirt with them. We can smile at them. We can keep short accounts. We can honor them. We can share our immediate experiences with them. We can stay connected from a distance! If we learn how to use these tools in the pursuit of transparency, then we can keep our connections tight in spite of time and distance.

Don't misunderstand me—I'm not suggesting that any of these tools are a good substitute for physically being together. They will merely help you stay attached when you have to be apart. When you don't have to be apart, then you really have to be *together*. What I mean is that when you are together, you must be available to one another. You may have things to accomplish but you are doing them as one. You may have children to rear or tasks to finish but you are single-hearted in them. You may have to pay attention to other things but you are always anticipating time to reconnect. Not only are you anticipating it, but you're also scheduling it.

In our time-demanding society, we have to purposefully slow down and gaze at one another. Put hard and fast time blocks into your schedule for lingering with one another. Schedule enough of them so you can catch the best part of each other's energy cycles. Time blocks scheduled when one or both of you are exhausted won't be as pleasant as they should be. They might even become stressful. Put them in places of optimum rest and peace, then savor them. For example, instead of disappearing into the garage or workshop for your regular alone time, schedule an hour or two to spend together. Hire a babysitter if needed. Then be together doing anything. You might be sacrificing your pet project but you are building something much more valuable.

If formerly disconnected couples can practice these few things and add to them as the Lord gives light, then they are giving themselves the best opportunity to stay connected for a lifetime. Remaining transparent requires meticulous attention. Once you create scrupulous habits of loving one another through transparency, you will become true reflections of the pure joy that awaits us in the arms of our Father and you will most likely be happier and healthier in this life.

Chapter 15

Master the Art

Men, now that you can connect, you must. Not only with your wife and your children, but also with every other man who remains in the clutches of disconnection. It is said that to teach something is to truly master it. We must become masters of connection, which means we must instruct those whom God places within our influence. Your sons are probably first in line, regardless of their age. If they are older, they probably learned your old disconnected patterns and need to travel a similar path to yours. If they are younger, you have the opportunity to prevent disconnection from taking root in their hearts.

You must lead out of the disobedience of disconnection anyone whom God places within your influence.

You have found and traveled a path that leads to salvation

and life. You have scaled walls of doubt and pain and watched as the bastions of your emptiness have been torn down. You have hacked a path through tangled jungles of old emotional stagnation and cleared connecting trails to those you love. You have no choice but to share your wisdom and knowledge with others. Your life is ransomed and your duty is clear—use your freedom in the pursuit of releasing others.

The first step, of course, is to ask God who is next to be freed. He will put someone in front of you and make it obvious what you are to do. You will have to prepare, though. Your preparation could be as simple as writing a few thoughts down about your journey. It might be as complex as writing a book. Whatever God calls you to do to prepare to lead others into connection, you must do. There are too many lives at stake for you to shirk this duty. Remember that it's not just the man's heart at risk. It's his wife, and his children, and their children. It is generations. Your obedience could mean a sea change for a hundred generations to come.

But let me be clear: You cannot refuse. To refuse is to disconnect, and to disconnect is to disobey. One heart set free can change the world.

Once prepared, you will have to practice. Keep constant diligence to exercise your connections daily. Stay linked and woven. Seek out connections. Invite more relationships. Think often of this duty. Implement, apply, and practice often to work out its best effect. Become a master of relationship in the image of the Master of relationship.

Now that you have won the hill, you must plant your flag and rally others to you. The hill is the ability to have loving relationships. It's the ground that, once won, must never be surrendered. The enemy cannot be allowed to have this hill. This is sacred ground. This is holy and priceless. It must be held even if it costs you your life. This hill is worth dying for.

Your passion for connection has to be infectious. You've spent long hours fighting to feel something. Keep the fires of those feelings stoked and tended. Fan them into a blaze that affects others. Reach out and pull as many as you can into the circle of warmth that radiates from the fire God has lit within you. I don't believe you can maintain the fire unless the fire is useful for others. I believe your new ability to connect will falter and smolder to spent embers if you don't fuel it by freeing others.

Now is the time to be a hero. Our society is crumbling under the weight of its own isolation. There are leagues of men going about their days in echo chambers of seclusion. They interact only to accomplish a task. They look out at the world through dirty and disfigured lenses. They brush aside gestures of gentleness and they scowl at overtures of love. They run to the blackened walls of their safe and impenetrable vaults. They are dying a black death of loneliness—they can't even taste the poison.

It's time for men who know their own frailty to stand up and fight. It's time for humble men to brawl with the enemy. It's time for good men to refuse defeat. It's time for honorable men to struggle and die for something worthwhile. It's time for you and me to lay down our lives to rescue and free the men of our age from the disease of our age. It's time to battle this raging foe of disconnection until we drive its furious malice back and listen as its beaten, anguished, and dying groans are heard slinking out of our land, never to return. I'm suited up; join me!

Thus says the LORD to you, "Do not fear or be dismayed because of this great multitude, for the battle is not yours but God's." (2 Chronicles 20:15b)

The LORD does not deliver by sword or by spear; for the battle is the LORD's and He will give you into our hands. (1 Samuel 17:47b)

For we wrestle not against flesh and blood, but against principalities, against powers, against the rulers of the darkness of this world, against spiritual wickedness in high places. Wherefore take unto you the whole armor of God, that ye may be able to withstand in the evil day, and having done all, to stand. (Ephesians 6:12–13 KJV)

But in all these things we overwhelmingly conquer through Him who loved us. (Romans 8:37 NASB)

Join with me by joining with others. Use this book for a men's or women's study group. Introduce it to your church or small groups pastor. Invite someone into a one-on-one exploration of what it means to connect. The best way to break a pattern is to consistently engage in a new one. Breaking out of disconnection requires connection.

Every man is a leader. Every man is an example for good or bad. Becoming a leader for good and for connectivity means overcoming our denials. It means *doing* something. We are doers by nature, if you remember, and it's one of the strongest qualities of a disconnected man. Use that strength to do the right thing.

If you need a place to start, it might help you to imitate the steps I took. Here's a snapshot of what I did when I started my path out of disconnection. I still do many of these things to stay connected.

STEP ONE

I connected with my Heavenly Father. I let Him love me and bend me. He was always gentle, but painfully firm. He will do the same for you. He let me feel lonely during long, sleepless nights when all I wanted to do was escape my pain. I wanted to run back to my disconnected comfort but He kept me awake, thinking, feeling, and suffering. But never allowing me to think He didn't love me.

STEP TWO

After suffering what I needed to suffer alone, I connected with good men. I met with three or four men per week, individually, and let them say anything they needed to say to me. I listened and worked hard to incorporate their lives into mine. It wasn't easy. I made a lot of mistakes. Below is a short synopsis of how those relationships went and a snippet of what I learned from each. I have benefited from these friends in countless ways.

Stephen

Stephen is one of the most gentle and gracious men I have ever met. He is truly kind and transparent. He strives for godliness. He honors friendship and remains loyal. He readily forgives and confesses. He doesn't hide anything.

We met nearly every week and worked through a discipleship curriculum together. The materials we used invited us to be intentional and honest about our walk with God. Stephen was honest in every detail. He shared with me when he failed and when he succeeded by God's grace. We prayed for one another often. Stephen witnessed my transition firsthand and encouraged me in every way.

When I met the lovely woman who was later to become my wife, he encouraged me. He was so excited to see what God was doing and took the time to counsel with me. He asked me the questions I needed to think about and answer. His wife was also a great help in giving me discernment as I navigated a relationship I really didn't expect to come along.

Stephen is the man who loved me no matter what. He walked with me no matter what. He encouraged and cheered for me no matter what. Stephen was truly enthusiastic for me and blessed me so that I could draw close to God. Having a man like Stephen to walk with made my path much easier than it could have been.

Matt

Matt is a velvet hammer. He loves deeply. He speaks sharply. He is as bold as a lion. He wrestles with the darkness. Sometimes his wrestling makes him dark. He can appear on the horizon like a foreboding storm cloud. He can drill through your granite composure with a point of his finger. He can encourage like no one else. He can rebuke like no one else.

Matt was the man most responsible for the miraculous transition I experienced. He was the hammer my hard head needed at the perfect time. He never minced words and he always told the truth as he saw it. Your friends should be truth tellers. They should be loyal. They should also be forgiving and full of grace. Matt has proven to be all of these and more.

Kevin

Kevin is an amazing guy. He looks gruff and scary but is gentle as a lamb to every good person and especially to those he loves. I met him because his wife was a part of a group I spoke to about being disconnected. She was so intrigued by my story that she wanted to read the manuscript of this book. She was certain that Kevin was just like me. She was right.

She shared part of my story with Kevin one night. She related how that went. He stormed out of the room, angry, only to return twenty minutes later in tears. Something she read had hit him squarely in the heart. He was stunned and believed that he needed to meet me. He was about to realize that he was a disconnected man.

We traded a few e-mails and set up a meeting. Kevin was surprised to meet a guy younger than him. He thought he would be meeting an older, wiser, gray-haired man who could guide him through his new discovery. What he got instead was a guy about his age, not very smart, only recently transformed by a lightning bolt of truth, and willing to share it with anyone who would listen. We became fast friends who understood one another.

When Kevin shares his experiences, they mirror mine. What

he feels, what he thinks, and what God is doing to transform him, all sound like what I went through. We have a great time sharing stories, praying for one another, and encouraging one another. We are soldiers together in this "connection war." Kevin is truly excited about connecting and helping others. He works hard at everything. He is someone I can count on. My hope and prayer is that every man who reads this book will find a Kevin to share a similar experience with. When you do, you've struck gold.

Find good men. Seek them out. Connect with them. Don't make excuses.

STEP THREE

Along with these regular meetings with men, I spent a lot of time talking to my children, who were all adult or near-adult at the time. I have the very special delight of having two sensitive and connected adult daughters. What I learned from them could fill another book. My two sons are strong, one very connected and one not. I learned a truckload from each of them in their own way.

My son, who is less connected but is a deep thinker, related so many helpful, surprising, and wise thoughts that I admire and use. My kids continually encouraged me and respectfully reprimanded me when I fell back into my old ways. I credit them with much of my healing.

I gave all my kids permission to call me out when I exhibited my old patterns. They didn't hesitate to take me up on that. I remember my oldest daughter on several occasions saying, "You can't do that anymore, Dad." She had to suppress a lot of her own fears to be so blunt with me, but her loving reprimands were always well timed. She also taught me a lot about the intricacies of relationships. She understands people well. She helps me navigate personalities so I can address each person with the special attention they need and deserve.

My youngest son could cut through my defenses like a knife. He never let me make excuses. He stuck to his opinion about what was driving me, and he often hit the mark. He was fearless when it came to helping me become better. He interpreted what others were saying to me. I understand better what people mean because of him.

My youngest daughter was my sounding board. I asked her many questions. She is the most sensitive, the most intuitive. She could tell me about motives, friendships, moods, and a hundred other relational things. She didn't mind answering my questions and helping me understand the emotional perspectives of others. I'm able to better interpret what others are feeling because of her help.

Listen to your children. Watch their reactions to you. Ask them how they feel about who you are, who you are becoming. Let them speak honestly. Don't shut them down.

STEP FOUR

I remarried. To say that I feel connected to my wife is almost an insult—we are an emulsion. We are blended in ways I could never have fathomed as a disconnected man. Our connection overwhelms me at times.

Before I go any further, though, I think there's a temptation to address. I am not in any way advocating divorce and remarriage for anyone. I beg you to fight for your marriage and to connect with the woman who is fighting to connect with you. Stay with the one you loved enough to marry and rediscover that love. My remarriage story, I think, is incredibly rare. I am a recipient of the broadest and deepest of God's grace. I cannot thank Him enough for reaching down to me—it is my daily delight to say thanks to Him.

My new marriage is worthy of another book. I have experienced miracle after miracle in my relationship with my wife. I won't do justice to what God has done in my heart and hers. Suffice it to say that I'm experiencing everything, every connection, every relational delight, every pain, every challenge alongside and intertwined with my wife's soul. It is beautiful. And there is more to come.

STEP FIVE

I'm living a connected life daily. I try to feel things. I talk more. I observe and try to understand how people feel. I think about ways to reach other disconnected men. I spread the word every chance I get. This book is the start. I hope you've been challenged by it. I hope you are connecting. I hope you are becoming relational. If you need help, please connect with me.

For you, for your church, for your group, I am available as God allows. Reach out to me and let's connect. Until then—may God bless you as you obediently connect with God and man.

Remember that masters never stop practicing. "If I miss practicing one day, I know it; if I miss two days, my friends know it; and if I miss three days the public knows it" is a quote attributed to many great classical musicians, from Franz Liszt to Ignacy Paderewski. I think it applies. Fight to practice and then practice to fight this war. You battle to perfect your skills, and by doing so you will change all of your relationships for the better. Let down and you risk falling back into disobedience and disuse. Persist and you will show the world the heart of God.

Appendix

What Do the Questions in Chapter 5 Reveal?

I want to repeat that I am no psychologist, and to be honest, I don't think I'm even a very good counselor. I only have experience with my own heart and my observations of others. The questions below are ones that I asked myself and that helped reveal what was going on inside. I offer comments for each to help you know what I'm getting at with the question. The Holy Spirit is the true counselor. If He puts His finger on any of these questions, then my advice is to listen to what He says and then take action on the information.

— *Do you now or have you ever felt deeply intertwined with anyone, in the sense that you really couldn't live without them?* This is not a question aimed at our intentions or our thoughts about someone. It is aimed directly at our hearts.

We may convince our minds that there is someone we couldn't live without, but we may be simply trying to comply with what is expected instead of what is reality. It's important to get beyond what is expected and answer honestly. Can we walk away from relationships without lasting pain?

If we can then, the reality is that we are probably disconnected in a harmful way. We are walking in disobedience to the relational commands of God. We are actively robbing loved ones and probably our Lord. We are keeping ourselves from them in order to protect our emotional fortress.

— *Do a lot of people consider you to be very competent at what you do?* This question is designed to reveal how we may have substituted achievement for connection. Those who are not emotionally connected still have needs for relationship. Often those needs are met when others see how competent they are—how much they can do. Interpersonal connection happens when achievements are complimented and rewarded. We feel as close as we ever do when someone acknowledges our successes.

This, unfortunately, is another substitute for obedient intimacy with God and others. God doesn't need us to do anything for Him. He simply wants us to abide in Him. Abiding is relating. Our wives, children, and loved ones are much the same. They don't primarily care what we can do for them—they want us to draw our souls close to them.

— *Have you been a natural overachiever most of your life? In other words, has success come easily, almost effortlessly, to you?* When we substitute achievement for relationship, we generally get very good at achievement. All our energies are working toward success in what we do, so we naturally become competent in those things. Our ability to easily overachieve may be an indicator of just how relationally disconnected we are. Years of *doing* instead of *feeling* add up to considerable expertise. Once we divert some of those achievement energies into relationships, we may find that our desires for success change in a drastic and wonderful way—especially for those who have longed to really know us.

— *Do you have fond memories of tender moments with your parents?* I'm asking to help us track disconnection to the source. I believe that there are many men who disconnect before they ever learn how to connect. Broken homes, parenting flaws, absent parents, tragedies, and the like can have serious and long-term effects. If we didn't connect tightly to our parents, then we may not have developed the equipment to connect to others.

— *Did you have a lot of dating relationships and breakups before you found your wife?* Having many dating relationships may be proverbial in our modern Western culture, but I think it has significance. If we dated to find love and companionship, then we probably gave parts of our hearts away to those we didn't form lasting bonds with. While dating and breakups may not have been the sources of our disconnection, they may have reinforced the subconscious conviction that we really didn't need to feel loved, that we could live without it.

— *How long did it typically take to recover from a breakup?* This question should reveal a very important dynamic about our emotional absorbency. If we can bounce back from emotional turmoil quickly and without much grief, then we may have a heart that is capable of rejecting even the emotions we should be absorbing and feeling. Hurt doesn't penetrate and stick like it should if we are nonrelational. Separation should hurt—if it doesn't, then let it be a red flag for you.

— *Have you ever had a very close friend or family member die? What was their name?* This is another question to test your ability to recover from loss. It has much the same application as the previous two questions. The death of a loved one should affect us deeply and for a length of time. If we recover quickly and grieve little, then we are most likely relationally stunted and disconnected.

— *How long did you grieve?* See explanation above.

— *Do you feel a hole in your heart where they used to be?* Pay close attention here. This question is another one we can't answer with what is expected. Our societal sensibilities want us to say, "Yes, of course I have a hole in my heart." Is that the honest answer? Is a part of you now forever missing because you lost this person, or do you feel wholehearted and fine without them?

— *Do you spend much time reminiscing about the past, or do you usually move on and look to the future?* This question is meant to explore your relational aptitude. Relational people love to reminisce and enjoy the memories of their connections. They recount and replay significant events, good and bad feelings, and loving connections. It fills them up. It strengthens the connections. Disconnected people are always "in the moment" and pushing ahead. Memories have very little value for them. In fact, they may not have very many of them because successes don't leave deep tracks in their hearts and they don't have relational tracks to follow.

— *Do overtly emotional movies or stories deeply affect you?* Why this question? If disconnected people don't feel deep emotions for others, then why would a movie or story affect them? The truth is that disconnected men DO have strong emotions but they are buried very deep. Once those emotions are touched, they are almost uncontrollable. Overly emotional stories can touch those sentiments hidden in the abyss, and when they do, the floodgates often open. This is very uncomfortable for an otherwise emotionally controlled man. He typically doesn't want anything to do with this level of unrestricted feeling. It is foreign, painful, debilitating, and intensely vulnerable—all things that scare him to death. It's a good indicator that his practice of control is keeping him disconnected.

— *What was happening the last time you broke down emotionally and cried?* This question is meant to invite you to ponder what touches you. If it was hard to remember the last time you were emotional to the point of tears, then it's probably worth meditating upon. What was the emotion? What was the event, the nature of the initial emotional touch? What did you feel? How long did it last? How did you respond to the emotion afterward? Take time to dissect what brought the emotion to the surface and what you did with it. It will help you learn to feel other emotions—especially relational ones.

— *Does change bother you?* This question is intended to make you think of how much you attach to people, places, or things. Can you easily leave a job, a person, a home, or any other thing that people often get attached to? There's nothing hard and fast indicated if you can, but it may be another indicator that you are someone who is more prone to disconnection than others.

— *Are you able to walk away from friends without staying in touch?* This was the arrow that pierced my heart. Without knowing it, I was capable of leaving nearly any relationship behind without a lot of angst. This question is intended to invite us to review our friendships and other relationships over our lifetime. Do you have old friends? Do you keep in touch? Do you think about them much?

— *Do you ever truly miss anyone? Is it a rare feeling to miss someone? I'm not asking if you ever feel lonely—I'm asking if you sincerely miss a special person.* Missing someone is feeling a loss. When we can feel a loss, we are more relational. I would go as far as to say that the ability to feel the pain of loss is essential to being a relational person. If you can connect with this pain, then you are getting closer to intimacy and making true relational progress. If it's difficult to feel loss, then it may be very difficult for you to feel connected.

— *Is it easy for you to leave a job and move on to another?* We covered this under the change question but it's worth revisiting. How easy is it for you to move on?

— *Are you passionate about your wife?* This is a big one. What am I asking? It may be difficult for you to even grasp the intention. Is your relationship pleasing and comfortable and stale, with nothing going on to rock the boat? Or is your relationship a fire in your heart? Does it energize and drive you? Does the thought of spending time with your wife ignite your mind and make you look forward to her company? I'm am not talking about sex here, men—I'm talking about passion for her person. Is she the flame that keeps your hearth warm? Do you ever even think about it? If not, it's time you do.

— *Does your love for your wife overcome you sometimes?* Ditto to the question above. Keep meditating on this. Do you think thoughts of His bride occupy the mind of Christ the groom? You bet they do—read your Bible. He talks constantly about His bride. Remember that love is not shown by doing things in a vacuum of feeling. Love is the overwhelming feeling that gives birth to doing. If we are simply doing as a substitute for feeling, we are most likely letting our bride down, and we are definitely not connecting with her.

— *Has anyone told you they thought you were proud (or arrogant)?* What does pride have to do with disconnection? Disconnection, at its root, is the habit of self-sufficiency. Self-sufficiency is pride. If others see us as prideful men, then we must pay attention. Pride, as with many other sins, is the root of disconnection. It is the sin of needing no one. This militates against everything in the Bible. God calls out to us to be the source and maintainer of love in our relationships—first of all with Him and then with family, all believers, and then the world. Humble men seek to serve and love others. Proud, disconnected men shy away from others.

— *If you have children, is it hard to leave them when you have to be away?* Again, don't give the expected answer. Be honest. Can you go on a business trip and barely think of your kids? The ability to lose sight of your flesh and blood is a sign of a disconnected heart. The lack of feeling sadness over lost time with them is yet another red flag. I'm not saying that we don't need a break sometimes. I am saying that if you can bury yourself in doing things without a thought for your family, you may be in the danger zone.

— *Do you get irrationally angry from time to time?* Those who know you can better address this question. You are capable of excusing yourself. What I'm getting at is that your ability to bury emotions related to connecting means you can probably bury your emotions related to relational frustration—at least for a time. Frustrations build and then often explode. Couple buried feelings and frustrations with pride, and the mix is as volatile as nitroglycerin. If you have a wife or family member who continues to push you to connect and engage in relationship, you may be experiencing ever-increasing frustration. Their insistence and your inability can become a toxic mix for you. The pressure builds over time and then someone pushes the red button and you react in ways you are likely to regret.

— *Describe the relationship you've had with your mom and dad.* This is another visit to the source. It pays to keep asking to see if you can dig up any evidence for early disconnection. It can help you forgive yourself and patch together a start on a new approach. Realizing that we are a product of many influences helps us know what to talk to the Lord about. He can heal all the flaws and missteps of your past and give you a new start.

— *Describe the relationship with your wife from YOUR perspective.* My explanations to the other questions above are probably enough to help you understand why I ask this one. It is extremely helpful to think about this. You may never have tried before. I encourage you to get alone with God and ask His help on this one. Write down everything He brings to mind. Think hard and meditate on the details that present themselves. This is a question designed to help you start connecting.

— *Describe your relationship with your wife from HER perspective.* This question may be the most difficult of them all. It is designed to get you to go into her mind and heart. It is a very frightening venture. IF you can explore deeply into this foreign territory, then I want to give you some very important news—you are well on your way to connecting with your wife. IF you are accurate with your description, then please know that you are very close to becoming the man who can give your wife what she has always longed for. You are very close to connecting. You are deliciously close to intimacy. You are delightfully close to seeing God's face and the inner sanctum of your wife's heart. Once there—you will never want to turn back.

— *Do you find it a bit irritating to answer these questions and think in this way?* Connected people love questions like this. Disconnected people get impatient with them. Which are you? Don't hesitate to review these questions and keep them handy for later. Disconnected men may have to revisit these questions numerous times to establish habits of relationship.

Acknowledgments

A great big thank you to all who helped me on this journey to connection and those who have helped me tell the story.

Thank you, Heavenly Father, for waiting for me and letting me know you think I'm worth it.

Thank you, Matt Jacobson, Tony Sprando, Stephen Williams, Scott Casteel, Dennis Hatchett, and Kevin Canaday—all godly men who helped me along the way.

Thank you to Michael Chaney, who shepherded my soul into truth without apology or pressure. Your wisdom is seen best from farther down the path.

Thank you to Lisa Jacobson, who suggested the audience and made the entire book come together.

Thank you, Kelsey, Tim, Robyn, and Levi for enduring everything—you are precious to me.

Thank you to my first wife. I'm sorry for the pain I caused.

Thank you to J. P. Brooks, my faithful brother, who did an amazing job editing my first draft. This book is so much better because of you.

Thanks to Don Jacobson and the D. C. Jacobson Agency for taking a chance on this book. Thanks to Tawny Johnson of the D. C. Jacobson Agency for coaching me through the grueling proposal process. You are a determined drill sergeant with a clear focus—exactly what I needed.

Thanks to Hachette Book Group and FaithWords for partnering with me to share my story. Thanks to Keren Baltzer of FaithWords for catching the vision and championing the book. Thanks for your edits and improvements. You have added depth and clarity where my thoughts and words were lacking. Thanks also to Grace Johnson for your faithful assistance.

Thanks to my incredible wife. You have taught me more about being connected than I thought I could ever know. You have my heart. We are one.

About the Author

JIM TURNER has been in youth or pastoral ministry for over twenty-five years and has personally experienced the pain and damage caused by disconnection. He is divorced as a direct result of his former disconnection, father of four incredible young adults, and now remarried and living in the delight of being truly connected with his wife. He has individually fought the battle to overcome disconnection and has entered into rich and fruitful relationships that reflect the commands of Christ for intimacy with Him and His followers. He "gets it" now and wants everyone else to join him!

Jim is also the author of *So-Called Christian* and coauthor of the *discipleme* discipleship workbooks (and soon to be released app) based on the need for disciple leaders to develop connected relationships with disciples rather than simply teaching them lessons.

Jim; his wife, Tanya; and their blended family of ten children (only seven still at home!) live in the beautiful Pacific Northwest. They enjoy music, theater, beach trips, great food, entertaining friends and family, and most of all being together!